LAKE VYRNWY

LAKE VYRNWY

THE STORY OF A SPORTING HOTEL

Revised and Updated Edition

John Baynes, George Westropp
and Simon Baynes

Quiller

© The Literary Estate of Sir John Baynes, Bt, George Westropp
and Simon Baynes

First published in 1992 by Sir John Baynes, Bt, and G. V. Westropp

Revised edition published in the UK in 2019
by Quiller, an imprint of Quiller Publishing Ltd

British Library Cataloguing-in-Publication Data
A catalogue record for this book is available from
the British Library

ISBN 978 1 84689 298 1

All photographs courtesy of Lake Vyrnwy Hotel and the Baynes and
Moir families unless otherwise stated.

Printed in Malta.

Quiller
An imprint of Quiller Publishing Ltd
Wykey House, Wykey, Shrewsbury SY4 1JA
Tel: 01939 261616
Email: info@quillerbooks.com
Website: www.quillerpublishing.com

Contents

Dedicated to the staff of Lake Vyrnwy Hotel, both past and present, without whose courtesy and hard work it could not be the happy place it is, and always has been.

Preface

ONE warm afternoon in late May 1991, I sat in a boat pulled up on Mrs Morris's Beach looking down Lake Vyrnwy through the haze towards the Tower. I started to muse on the massive endeavour to build the Lake in the first place and the impact on an ancient and close-knit community of being uprooted and transported down the valley below the dam. I considered how much the Hotel had changed in just my lifetime and all the different proprietors and guests coming and going over the century since 1890.

Countless thousands of fishers had drifted past that very beach in all seasons and weather over the last century, while the moors and woods echoed each year to the guns after grouse and pheasant.

Vyrnwy is a special place, I concluded, and it really was time for somebody to write a book about it all.

But, in fact, it was the Hotel's previous owner, Sir John Baynes, who took the initiative. He called me about just such an undertaking a few months later, and we began the process that led to the publication of *Lake Vyrnwy: The Story of a Sporting Hotel* in 1992.

Nearly thirty years on, the late Sir John's son Simon Baynes sent me an email asking whether it was not time to revisit the book. The Hotel has been transformed during those years; there is a new generation in the valley and even the sporting side has been changed by the outdoor pursuit interests of the Hotel guests and visitors.

There was no doubt in my mind that the book needed a complete update and Simon Baynes, therefore, took up the challenge with the help of the Hotel's general manager, Anthony Rosser, and the managing director, Brian Bisiker. Brian's family now owns the Hotel and the sporting rights on the Vyrnwy

Estate. There were many others in and around Llanwddyn who have kindly provided their insights and wisdom to assist in the re-writing of the original book and Simon and I are grateful to them all.

In 1973, I wrote a booklet on fishing Lake Vyrnwy, which included the following foreword by Simon's grandfather, Sir Roy Baynes, when he was living with his family at the Hotel. We still cannot think of a more suitable passage to introduce a book about the Lake Vyrnwy Hotel.

'After nearly fifty visits to Lake Vyrnwy, as one comes over the top of the hill above Llanwddyn, down around the hairpin bend, then up again to the Lake, one finds the feeling of excitement and anticipation as strong as ever. A short stop by the dam to see the water level and direction of the wind, and then on up to the Hotel. Unpack, get into fishing clothes and out on to the Lake and get an hour or so before it's time to come in for dinner. Then back to the Hotel to change, and before going into the dining room a little time in the bar, and a chance to look at the fish laid out in the trays in the hall. But why after so many years does one look forward to it so much? First, of course, there is the fishing. This book will tell you all about that. Nowhere have I had so many friends, and nowhere can I be so sure of meeting them again, year after year. In the *Compleat Angler*, Izaak Walton, when describing how to cook a pike with oysters and a variety of other succulent ingredients, wrote: "This dish of meat is too good for any but anglers and very honest men." I would para-phrase Izaak Walton and say: Lake Vyrnwy is too good for any but anglers and very friendly men – and women too, of course!'

George Westropp, April 2019

PART 1

How it Came About

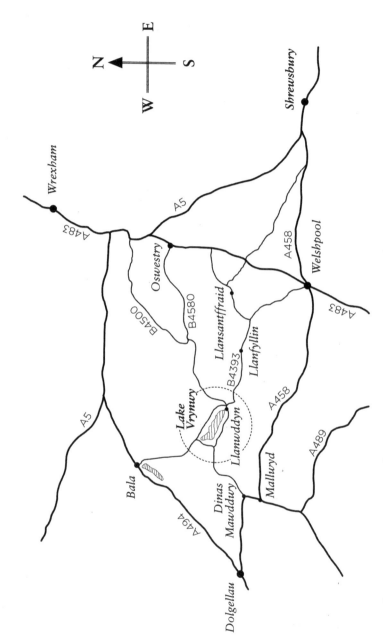

The general location of Lake Vrynwy showing main approach roads

CHAPTER ONE

The Valley in the Days Before the Lake

THE creation of Lake Vyrnwy was a massive endeavour, which ranks as one of the greatest feats of engineering in the Victorian era. The magnificent dam, built from local stone, was at the time the largest masonry dam in Europe and the Lake is to this day the largest expanse of water in Wales. To do this justice, a start must be made with a short description of the valley before the Lake was created. Fortunately, a very active vicar was appointed to the parish of Llanwddyn in 1870, who busied himself collecting a mass of information about his parish and the village at the centre of it. In 1873, the Reverend Thomas H. Evans published his findings in Volumes VI and VII of the *The Montgomeryshire Collections*, part of a great store-house of the local history regularly produced from 1868 up to the present day.

As part of his description of the scenery, Evans quoted from an essay written by one T. W. Hancock, who from his narrative must have come to the valley from the north-west, following the road from Penybontfawr.

'At Abermarchnant the vale has the character of a pass, and is very contracted, in some places not more than a couple of chains lengths across, the hills on either side are pretty and well wooded. Near Cynon-isaf [the farm on which the Hotel now stands] it expands where a broad flat opens to view, which is bounded by the mountains of Eunant and Rhiwargor. The average width of the vale may be about three quarters of a mile, and its extent about six miles. The flatness from the village to Eunant, to an eye untrained in observing natural beauties, would be uninteresting, on account of the morass-like nature of the ground, which is also broken up by many channels. But the tourist will be more than compensated when he enters the inlet by Rhiwargor, for here the scenery is at once changed as if by a magician's wand, and he is in the midst of scenery grand in point of colour, boldness and breadth, and picturesque by its roughness and contrast of foliage and rock, cascade, etc.'

To this Evans added his own comment on the view to be obtained from the high ground above and to the west of Llanwddyn village:

'The scenery is not entirely confined to the upper end of the parish, for in standing on the north-east of St John's hill looking north, we find the beautiful little valley of Cedig, with all its variety of objects, spread before us, the hills on each side covered over with heather, and divided into kind of semi-circles by the green dingles and the bright rivulets that pass along them, and nowhere can the eye be tired with sameness.'

Apart from the obvious absence of the Lake, the main difference that an eye accustomed to the view of the area today would notice would be the freedom of the hills from the great belts of conifers, which now cover so many of them. The fields in the valley rose up to meet open heather moorland on all sides, and such woodland as existed was all broadleaf, mainly sessile oak. On the moors, grouse were plentiful, while a wide range of birds were found on the lower ground. As well as all the more common small birds there were red kites and other raptors, and grey partridges were seen in the cultivated fields. Fish in the river were mainly trout and chub, with the occasional salmon.

Given the heavy annual rainfall in the area it is not surprising that there was everywhere an abundance of water, both flowing down from the hills in the streams, and filling the marshes along the course of the River Vyrnwy in the valley bottom. Evans reported that 'one third of the vale remained under water in the winter' and was useless for agriculture. The only crops this bog produced were rushes, interspersed with occasional alder and willow groves.

The village of Llanwddyn, which lay roughly half-way up the valley at the foot of the Afon Cedig, or Cedig River, took its name from an early Saint named Wddyn (pronounced 'Oothin') who was reported to have lived as a recluse in a nearby cave in the sixth century. Although the parish was also designated Llanwddyn, its church was named after St John of Jerusalem. The reason for this was that in the thirteenth century the manor of Llanwddyn had come into the hands of the Knights Hospitaller (Knights of the Order of St John of Jerusalem), who had built a stone church in the village and dedicated it to their patron saint.

The parish of Llanwddyn, which extended over all the land today lying beneath the Lake, plus the hills surrounding it, covered 19,500 acres. This was made up of one thousand acres of cultivated land, 4,500 acres of meadow and pasture, four hundred acres of woodland, and 13,600 acres of unenclosed common land. In 1873, it was divided into fifty holdings: twenty-three of over one hundred acres, and twenty-seven of under one hundred acres. The main owners of the land, other than common land, were the Earl of Powis, Sir E. Buckley, Bt, and Sir Watkin Williams-Wynn. Between them, these three held just over five thousand acres. Among other owners were T. Storey who had 422 acres, Thomas Gill of Cynon-isaf with 182, and Mary Erasmus of Allt-Forgan with 175. The vicar's glebe itself extended to 73 acres.

At the time of the national census in 1871 the population of the parish was recorded as 433. Forty years earlier in 1831 this figure had been 668, or roughly one-third greater. The lure of higher wages in the expanding industries of north-west England and the Midlands had drawn many people away from their isolated homes in the valley. To accommodate the population, there were one hundred houses in the parish of which thirty-seven were in the village with ten farmsteads in the surrounding countryside. Evans specifically mentioned 'four principal ancient houses', which he named Eunant, Rhiwargor, Allt-Forgan, and Cynon-isaf, stating that '... these were occupied for generations by gentlemen having long pedigrees and high standing'.

Farming was the main occupation of the inhabitants of the valley. Crops grown included barley and oats, a small quantity of wheat, potatoes, swedes and turnips. This was all for home consumption by the people themselves, or as winter feed for stock. In earlier times, when the population had been bigger, more land had been cultivated, but over the years it had been found easier and cheaper to turn land over to pasture for grazing. Some cattle were kept, but the main attribute for which the area was well known was the fine type of Welsh mountain sheep bred there.

For fuel the inhabitants relied largely on peat, which was cut on the moors and carted or pulled on sledges down to the houses in the valley. This simple self sufficiency was reflected in the diet of the majority of the people, which consisted of mutton broth, porridge, gruel, and milk. That such an apparently harsh way of life could be a remarkably healthy one can be demonstrated by the longevity of many of the inhabitants in days when the average expectation of life in the rest of Britain was far below what it is today. Evans reported twenty-one persons in the parish of over seventy-five years of age in 1870, of whom one was 102. Cases of others reaching one hundred were recounted to him from previous years.

Like all communities in isolated rural areas at the time, the people of Llanwddyn retained many old superstitions and beliefs from far back in history. Fear of ghosts and evil spirits was still prevalent, heightened by the occasional appearance over the bogs by the river of a 'will-o'-the-wisp'. This phenomenon is a light caused by spontaneous combustion of methane, or marsh gas, produced in water-logged ground. Primitive anxieties about the supernatural were somewhat at variance with the strong religious influences in the parish, there being three denominations of non-conformists with chapels in the village as well as the Church of St John.

Not many visitors came to Llanwddyn in the days before the Lake was made. The few who did stayed in the Powis Arms hotel in the village, and were mostly men coming for the grouse shooting. One member of a shooting party, who had a very exciting experience in 1875 while staying in the village, was a Mr Richard Blakeway-Phillips, from Hanwood in Shropshire. A newspaper report tells how a 'water spout', or cloudburst, struck the valley, and in a few minutes the whole village was inundated:

'The school was completely isolated by the surging waters, and a number of the children who were in it were compelled to climb upon the forms and window sills to escape drowning. Throughout the village the greatest possible excitement prevailed, and the utmost anxiety was naturally felt for the safety of the children. Fortunately, however, Mr Blakeway-Phillips of Hanwood, Shrewsbury, who happened to be staying at the inn, heard of the perilous position in which the little folks were placed, and he at once volunteered, if a rope could be obtained, to go to their rescue.

The current was flowing very rapidly, but he succeeded

in crossing it. The landlord of the inn endeavoured to follow, but the rope broke, and he was washed back to the side from which he started. Upon reaching the school, which was surrounded by water to a depth of several feet, the gentleman broke open the windows, and with the assistance of a man who reached the school about the same time from another direction, the children were got out and taken to places of safety. A few minutes after the last child was removed, the building, which was erected on peaty soil, collapsed, and it was evident that had not assistance been very promptly rendered, all the children must have perished.

The many currents which rushed down from the neighbouring hills washed up the gravestones in the yard, and carried away several yards of the wall. Mr Phillips had to wait for upwards of an hour for the waters to subside before he could venture to return, and when he did so, the bridge over which he had crossed also gave way. The vicar of the parish, the Rev. T. H. Evans, the schoolmaster, and the inhabitants of the village generally expressed their gratitude to Mr Phillips and others, who they felt had been first and foremost in rendering the assistance which proved so effectual.'

Isolated, peaceful, and rarely visited though it might still be as the 1870s progressed, the upper Vyrnwy valley was, by virtue of its shape and geological base, of interest to a distant body of people who were, before long, to make a massive impact on the lives of all who lived there. This body was the City Council of Liverpool, and the concern of its members was to find a site for a new reservoir to provide more water for the ever-expanding population of the great sprawling urban area they controlled along the banks of the Mersey. Various sites were under consideration in northern England and Wales, but in most cases some snag prevented them from being suitable.

In the summer of 1877 Mr Deacon, the city engineer of Liverpool, arrived in Llanwddyn to investigate the possibility of damming the River Vyrnwy at a point somewhere below the village to create a large artificial lake capable of holding many millions of gallons of water. During his surveying of the area, a rock bar was discovered lying across the bed of the valley at the point where it began to narrow two miles south of the village. The potential of this rock bar as a base on which to construct a dam convinced Deacon that he had at last discovered a good site for the creation of a reservoir.

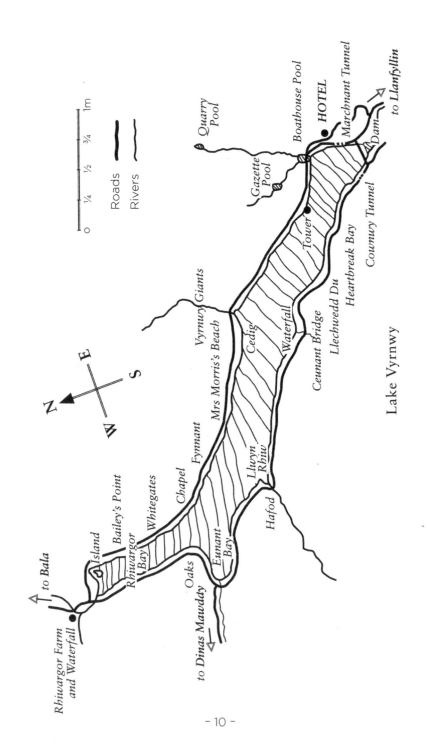

Lake Vyrnwy

Roads
Rivers

0 ¼ ½ ¾ 1m

N E S W

to Bala

Rhiwargor Farm
and Waterfall

to Dinas Mawddy

to Llanfyllin

Island
Bailey's Point
Rhiwargor Bay
Whitegates
Chapel
Fynnant
Oaks
Eunant Bay
Hafod
Llwyn Rhiw
Mrs Morris's Beach
Vyrnwy Giants
Cedig
Waterfall
Ceunant Bridge
Llechwedd Du
Heartbreak Bay
Tower
Cownwy Tunnel
Dam
HOTEL
Marchnant Tunnel
Boathouse Pool
Gazette Pool
Quarry Pool

CHAPTER TWO

Creating the Lake

As Liverpool City engineer, Deacon was investigating the possibility of building a dam in the valley of the River Vyrnwy because of the problems the city was experiencing in obtaining enough water for its ever-increasing population. What had been a small town at the beginning of the eighteenth century had become, by the middle of the nineteenth, a sprawling city with administrative responsibilities not only for Liverpool and Bootle, but for such areas as Crosby, Aintree, Kirkby, Huyton, and Halewood: in fact, for the whole of north Merseyside. By the 1840s, the water supply had become totally inadequate, so in 1847, following an Act of Parliament, a large reservoir was constructed twenty-eight miles away at Rivington in Lancashire, from where water was piped to the city. Further small reservoirs were built in the following years, but by 1865 the increase in demand had overtaken the capacity of the new supplies. Public health had much improved when the water from Rivington had first become available but as the demand once again exceeded supply a general deterioration in health was noted. By 1866 it was clear that a new source of water had to be found.

Deacon's predecessor, a Mr Duncan, had reported on a number of sites for the construction of a new reservoir in the Lake District and north Wales. He personally favoured a scheme involving Lake Bala and the River Tryweryn, which joins the River Dee just below it. Matters were then delayed by Duncan's death. The construction of a new railway caused Deacon, his successor, to report in due course that the Bala scheme was no longer possible. Consideration was given in 1874 to more schemes in Lancashire and the Lake District, but it was not until 23 July 1877 that Deacon was instructed to report on the possibilities of the Vyrnwy valley. In contrast to the rather dilatory approach to the problem of the preceding eleven years, Deacon now worked more swiftly, and presented his report on 27 November that year. It was accepted in principle, and in September 1878 trial shafts were sunk at the chosen site to see if the rock bed would provide a secure enough foundation on which to build a dam destined to hold back a head of water of ten thousand million gallons.

In 1880 the Liverpool Corporation Waterworks Act was passed by Parliament and received the Royal Assent on 6 August. Preparations were at once put in hand to gather the work-force and equipment necessary for the construction of what was to become the first large masonry dam in Britain and the largest artificial reservoir in Europe at the time. Work on the site began in July 1881, commemorated by a stone laid at the northern end of the dam on 14 July by the Earl of Powis. This can still be seen today, along with two others commemorating later stages of the work.

The stone for the masonry was obtained from the quarry specially opened up in the valley on the eastern side of what is now the Lake, the road to which branches right at the bottom of the Hotel drive. All other materials were brought by horse and cart from the railway station at Llanfyllin, ten miles away. Stabling for up to one hundred horses was built in Llanfyllin, where parts of the walls can still be seen, and at Llanwddyn. The road between the two places had to be improved, and at one point realigned to ease the gradient. The labour force topped one thousand men at the busiest stage of the work on the dam. Many of them were stonemasons working in the quarry, dressing the stone, which was not easy to handle.

In a remarkably short time, compared with that taken to reach a decision to build it, work on the dam was completed. The old village of Llanwddyn and all buildings in the valley that were due to be covered by water were demolished. A new church, dedicated to St Wddyn, had been built on a rocky spur of the hill on the north side of the new works. On 27 November 1888 this new church was consecrated, and the next day the valves at the base of the dam were closed. To general surprise the new Lake filled more rapidly than anticipated and, just under a year later, on 22 November 1889 the water flowed over the lip of the dam.

On the same hill as the church, a monument was erected in memory of ten men who were killed during the course of the building works, presumably due to accidents on the site, and a further thirty-four who died from other causes while construction was in progress. Given the average life expectancy for a manual labourer in those days this is not a surprising figure for a seven-year period.

The building of the dam was not the only engineering feat necessary for the provision of a water supply: equally vital was the creation of a suitable means of bringing it to Liverpool. The water's sixty-eight-mile journey to taps in the city started at the straining tower, designed to both strain it through huge wire-gauze filters and to regulate the level of draw-off. From the tower, often compared to a castle on the Rhine and such a well-known feature of the Vyrnwy landscape, the water passed to the start of a tunnel driven two-and-a-quarter miles up through the hillside in a north-easterly direction. The tunnel then connected at Hirnant to a forty-two-inch pipe, capable of carrying thirteen million gallons of water to Liverpool each day. Balancing reservoirs and filtration works were also set up along the route. On 14 July 1892 the first water flowed into the city.

Over the following years, further steps were taken to increase the amount of water that could be drawn off the Lake. By 1905, a second line of forty-two-inch pipe had been laid. A third was added in the 1920s and 30s. To augment the flow of water into the Lake itself, diversion dams were constructed in the beds of two streams that flow into the River Vyrnwy below the dam: the Marchnant on the north side, and the Cownwy on the south. From the small lakes created by these dams, tunnels were driven down to carry extra water into the Lake. The Cownwy tunnel comes out on the southern shore opposite the Hotel, and at times of heavy rain can be seen pouring out a huge foaming torrent into the Lake. The completion of these works in 1910 was marked by an official opening by the then Prince of Wales, later King George V, and the planting of a tree, which can be seen on the right of the road just beyond Pont Cynon, better known to visitors as the 'boat-house bridge', lying at the bottom of the Hotel drive.

A further building task was needed to re-house the people whose homes were demolished in the lead-up to the filling of the Lake. In keeping with the quality of the dam, handsome stone houses were erected on either side of the valley immediately below it, and these can still be seen and admired over a century later. Although there were at the time, and have been since, many people who have criticised the decision to flood the valley, the Lake's creation brought prosperity and stability to the area. During its long period of guardianship up to 1973, when the estate was passed into the hands of the Severn Trent Water Authority, the Liverpool Corporation proved to be a model landlord and employer. A clue to the benefits of this good care of the community can be demonstrated by the fact that the census of 1961 showed a population fall of only ten per cent from the 1871 figure, while the average drop in seven similar parishes in the surrounding area was fifty per cent.

While construction work was in progress, housing was required for the workmen on the site. Dr Hugh Jones, one-time surgeon to the Corporation, recorded in 1893 that '... two series of semi-detached wooden huts were erected, each hut consisting of a large living room, a store room, two small bedrooms, and a sleeping apartment for twelve men'. Although intended as purely temporary accommodation, some of these huts were still occupied by local people, who had moved into them, long after the dam had been completed.

In order to avoid disrupting the flow of the River Vyrnwy below the dam, arrangements had to be made to allow water to pass through valves at its base into the bed of the river. As well as the regular daily discharge, on four days a month, for eight months of the year, a big head of what was termed 'compensation water' was released into the river. The thrust of both these types of discharge passing though relatively narrow valves was so great that a decision was made to employ it to make electricity. A generating plant was installed in 1902, which continued to supply Llanwddyn village, the Corporation offices, and the Hotel with electricity until 1966, when Manweb brought a mains supply to the valley.

The enterprise of providing Liverpool with water embraced another whole range of responsibilities beyond the physical creation of the reservoir and the pipe lines leading from it. This was the purchase and management of land: both the land that was to be flooded, and also the extensive area forming the watershed that would drain into the new lake. To have full control of the watershed was especially vital in view of the intention that Vyrnwy should be a clean water reservoir, from which the water would flow untreated, except for normal filtration, directly into taps in Liverpool.

There is not space here to give more than the briefest account of the various stages in the process of purchasing the land that eventually made up an estate of 23,000 acres. Initially 13,415 acres were purchased out of a catchment area of 18,260. In due course the rest of the land in the catchment came into the hands of the Corporation. When the Marchnant and Cownwy diversionary dams and tunnels were built, more ground was bought up. A last purchase of land in 1930 brought the estate to its present size. The main sellers were the major landowners mentioned earlier in Chapter 1. The Earl of Powis retained the sporting rights over all the land he sold, as did Sir Watkin Williams-Wynn over part of the grouse moors in the parish of Llangynog. Mr Thomas Gill of Cynon-isaf used the money he received to extend his other house, called Brynderwen, lying twelve miles away near Llanfyllin. It was on Thomas Gill's land that the Hotel was built in due course.

Management of the estate during the early years was in the hands of Mr W. Forrester Addie of Welshpool, who was also agent for the Powis estates. The first resident agent at Vyrnwy was appointed in 1928. This was Mr Humphrey Howard, who remained in office for thirty-six years until retiring in 1964. A man of great ability and character, as well as possessing a fine sense of humour, Humphrey not only became 'uncrowned king' of Vyrnwy, but was for many years an important figure on the county council, first of Montgomeryshire, then Powys. In 1959, his step-son David Rowlands joined him as an assistant, following him as chief agent on his retirement. In 1979 David left to run his own farm, and was succeeded by Mr Michael Duggleby.

In a useful short book entitled *History and Description of Llanwddyn and Lake Vyrnwy*, from which much of the material for this chapter has been drawn, David Rowlands described how the Corporation ran the estate, and how the afforestation of the land around the Lake took place:

'The estate as purchased consisted almost entirely of tenanted farms more than two thirds of whose land was unenclosed mountain. Between 1890 and 1912 the Corporation planted about nine hundred acres with mainly coniferous plantations although in many areas about ten per cent of beech were included as a soil improver. During that period the Corporation were advised that it would be desirable to plant the slopes surrounding both the Lake and the lower parts of the main feeder streams, and in 1912 they entered into an agreement with the Development Commissioners to plant a further four thousand acres.

The First World War delayed the start of the additional planting but in 1920, in conjunction with the Forestry Commission, which had succeeded the Development Commissioners, work began.

Farms were taken in hand by the Corporation as and when they became vacant; the plantable land was planted and the mountain land was merged with farms managed by the Corporation. By 1936 the planting programme was completed and the Corporation were farming about eleven thousand acres of which all but six hundred acres were mountain land.

During the war of 1939–45 the country was desperately short of timber and much of the original nine hundred acres of the Corporation's plantations were felled, about sixty thousand tons of timber being produced from the estate during the war.'

What was left of the nine hundred acres of the Corporation's own plantations was sold in 1946 to the joint scheme with the Forestry Commission, and so became included with the four thousand acres under that shared control. The money raised was used to build the community centre, school, and village known as Abertridwr, the extensive and well-designed buildings of which are seen on the right of the road, soon after coming into the valley, on rounding the hairpin bend on the road from Llanfyllin.

Following the Water Act of 1973, Lake Vyrnwy and the estate passed from the control of Liverpool Corporation into that of the Severn Trent Water Authority in 1974. So that the water could continue to be used by Liverpool, an abstraction licence was granted to the North West Water Authority (part of United Utilities since 1995), which now looks after the city's interests, enabling it to draw off from the Lake. The management of the estate gradually changed under Severn Trent Water Authority with considerable alterations to the old paternal Liverpool Corporation style of operation. The workforce on the estate was greatly reduced with much forestry work being done by contractors, as opposed to the home-based forestry gang. Another major change in practice came in the mid-1980s, with the start of a policy of allowing the sale of houses and buildings to private purchasers: something always resisted fiercely by the Corporation. This change of estate management policy had an important influence on the history of the Hotel.

—∞—

CHAPTER THREE

Building the Hotel

THE decision to build a hotel beside the Lake was a natural development of the intention to create a new reservoir in an isolated valley sixty-eight miles from Liverpool, and ten miles from the nearest rail-head. The site made it difficult for anyone wishing to spend any length of time in the area of the Lake to do so without finding overnight lodging. The requirement for a hotel became obvious soon after the enterprise was launched. Before describing the categories of visitors expected to make use of it, it must be stressed how excited many people were all over Britain, as well as in other countries, at the news of the setting up of this massive engineering project. From the start it was clear that it would draw sightseers and other viewers in considerable numbers.

The first category of anticipated visitors comprised the members of the Liverpool Corporation, and other dignitaries from the city. To ensure that there would be rooms available for city councillors and officials when required, conditions were written into the terms of the lease of the Hotel that stipulated that accommodation had to be reserved for them at certain times of the year. Category two consisted of a wide range of people, mainly engineers, who were known to be interested in the construction of the dam, and the method of drawing water from the Lake. Both during the construction phase and long after the valley had been flooded, experts came from all over the world to study the techniques used in creating what was then, and for a long time, the biggest artificial lake in Europe. The third category of visitors for which the Hotel was built embraced a variety of private people, including those who would come to fish or shoot, walkers, naturalists, artists, and ordinary holiday-makers. Given the social conditions of the time, these early customers with sufficient money and leisure to spend several days or weeks at a spell away from home expected spacious accommodation, and, in many cases, to bring their own personal servants with them.

The site first chosen for the building of the Hotel was high on a hill at the northern end of the Lake, directly above the house and farm at Rhiwargor. It would have been a magnificent setting with splendid views, but had to be abandoned for an important but prosaic reason: since the aim was to preserve the water in the purest possible form, no sewage was permitted to find its way into the reservoir. From the rocky hillside where the Hotel might have been erected, no suitable way could be found of directing the sewage away from contaminating the Lake, and there was no possibility of siting a septic tank or filtration plant. Another site had to be found. The place finally selected provided almost as good a view of the waters as the original choice, and had three further advantages. It was easier of access, the sewage could be taken away via filter beds to a stream joining the River Vyrnwy below the dam, and it was in a drier area. Surprisingly, the rainfall at the northern end of the Lake, due to the surrounding hills, is ten or more inches higher than at the south in an average year.

The original building was smaller than the one that stands today with two lower, rather shed-like, structures beyond the main Hotel which housed the kitchen and usual domestic offices and stores. Beyond them again, the stone coach-house with a pinnacle on top also contained the farm bailiff's quarters. Further on, out of sight, were cow sheds and some excellent stabling, with four good loose boxes as well as stalls and a tack room. Although apparently well set up with all the varieties of accommodation and working areas required, it was not long before, as is so often the case with new places, these were found inadequate.

Around the turn of the century several cottages were erected. The best of these was a neat stone house, set in a secluded spot about a hundred yards north-east of the Hotel, which became known as the 'Eagle's Nest' and still stands today. There was also a row of four other workmen's cottages by the sheep pens at the far end of the field above the Hotel but they were later pulled down. The tenants found it necessary to put up a number of wooden buildings as well, mostly connected with the farm and the sporting facilities, which included extra cow houses, a gun room, overflow accommodation for servants, and a laundry. Another slightly surprising outbuilding to find in the grounds was the local post office, which was sited on the lawn just opposite the side entrance to the main Hotel.

In 1905 a major reconstruction of the main building was carried out. The early kitchen block was pulled down, and a long wing was added, stretching up towards the farm area. On the ground floor, a new kitchen and ancillary rooms were placed on one side of a central corridor; on the other was a large billiard room and a steward's room, occupying what is now the restaurant. Upstairs there were two floors of living accommodation adding approximately nineteen letting bedrooms to the fifteen in the earlier part of the building. In time this number would be increased, as private sitting rooms were converted to bedrooms.

The year 1930 saw the erection of a further extension at the end of the new wing. This added two bedrooms and a bathroom upstairs, and a steward's room and staff room below. At this point the billiard room disappeared, allowing it and the earlier steward's room to be opened up into one large dining room. The rooms that had earlier been used as dining rooms were re-designated as a drawing room and smoking lounge. There were still only a few bathrooms in the Hotel, and hot water was carried in brass cans to the bedrooms morning and evening by the chambermaids. Chamber pots were still in regular use, and the unfortunate chambermaids had the task of 'slopping' them out in the mornings.

Although the outer structure of the buildings was not greatly altered for the next sixty years, there were constant internal changes. In the late 1940s, hot and cold running water was piped to hand-wash basins in all bedrooms. One elderly permanent resident was so annoyed by this modern 'fad' that he departed, complaining bitterly at not having his brass can of hot water brought to his room. In the 1950s, four extra private bathrooms were provided, to make a total of six bedrooms with this increasingly demanded facility, to which were added a further five in the 1970s. In 1956, a major alteration to the tap room, or public bar, was put in hand. Until then it had been lodged in a fairly small and not very comfortable room at the back of the 1930 extension. To provide better premises, the building occupied by the farm bailiff's quarters and a coach-house was taken over, and what amounted to a separate local pub was created, with a spacious public bar and a smaller lounge bar overlooking the Lake. Further improvements were made in the 1970s and early 80s, with cooking facilities and a pool room added to what was now referred to as 'The Tavern', rather than 'the tap room'.

Following the change of ownership in the mid-1980s, the building underwent massive internal alterations in 1987, which have been followed by further developments to expand the Hotel and its facilities. More recent building work has been necessary to keep pace with changes in demand among customers. Today, a private bathroom with each bedroom is considered essential in any good hotel, while a hundred years ago affluent guests regarded private sitting rooms as more important. As the years have gone by, the changes in taste among visitors have caused the structure of the Hotel to be altered to suit them. What is unchanging, and perhaps its greatest asset, is the superb panorama of Lake and hills, which can be seen from its windows: a view that never fails to give pleasure whatever the mood of the weather.

PART 2

A History of the Hotel

CHAPTER FOUR

The First Fifty Years: 1890–1940

THE first tenant to take a lease of the newly built Hotel in 1890 was Mr G. Ward. The Liverpool Corporation was lucky to find a man who was clearly of considerable wealth, since he took over an empty building, which he had to furnish and set up with all fittings, other than those fixed fittings that were part of the premises. His outlay was seven thousand pounds on all these items, which in today's terms would be approaching £860,000. No doubt he was charged a low rent, but, with no established goodwill to go with the business, this would be the only commercial advantage in taking on the place. It would seem, however, that Ward was as much interested in the sporting rights offered with the lease as in the Hotel itself. Evidence of this can be found in the details of the first year's fishing on the Lake in 1891, which show him to have been the most successful individual fisherman of the season. To have time to pursue his own sporting interests, he employed a Mr W. Durant Gibbings to manage the Hotel for him, which was a considerable luxury in an establishment with only fifteen letting bedrooms, of which an unusually high proportion were singles. Before long the financial strain proved too much for him, and Ward decided to move on. He contrived to assign his lease in 1892 or 93 to Miss Davies, formerly joint proprietor of the Powis Arms in the drowned village, but suffered a loss of several thousand pounds.

Miss Davies was to remain at Vyrnwy for very much longer, though, in the end, to have little more financial success than her predecessor. She was a very capable woman, who ran a very comfortable hotel with a reputation for good food. Much of her trade came from visiting engineers and reporters for technical journals, who, in the early years, were constant arrivals to examine the wonders of the new dam and Lake. There were also figures from the Corporation to be put up during their frequent inspections of the new works. Other guests usually came for longish visits of up to a fortnight. Complete families often arrived, bringing their own personal servants. It can be assumed that the small bedrooms on the second floor were designed to be used by children and servants, while the parents had bedrooms and sitting rooms on the first floor. A diary dated 1896, discovered in the attic not long ago, showed relatively few bookings, but nearly all for longish visits.

No doubt with Miss Davies' full approval, and perhaps at her instigation, the new wing was added in 1905. This made the Hotel a potentially more profitable size, adding a further nineteen bedrooms to the original fifteen. Unfortunately, this addition was of little benefit to Miss Davies herself, who found the necessary outlay on equipping and furnishing the extension a serious drain on her resources. Within a few years she was anxious to surrender her lease, having for some time been trading at a loss. She attempted to sub-let the Hotel, but found no takers. Eventually, in 1909, a Mr William Hampson arrived on the scene, and it is from studying his correspondence that much of the story of these early days has been pieced together.

By trade, Hampson was a manufacturer of leather goods, owning a factory largely devoted to making harness and equipment for horse-drawn vehicles, still very much in demand until well into the twentieth century. His venture into the hotel business made him the proprietor of the inn at Pen-y-Gwryd, then, as now, a popular resort for mountain climbers. Both at Pen-y-Gwryd and Vyrnwy he employed managers to run the hotels for him, in the latter case a Mr Bennett. While taking a keen interest in both establishments, he was often away from them, staying at the house he owned at Betws-y-Coed. From

Pen-y-Gwryd he brought with him, to run the home farm as working bailiff, John Hill, the father of a large family, many of whom still live in or near Llanwddyn. Eventually there were nine Hill children: five girls and four boys. The family lived in the farm bailiff's house, which is today the site of The Tavern, the pub next to the Hotel. Several of the children were to work in various capacities for the Hotel as they grew up. Ruby, the eldest, was in charge of poultry and the dairy for many years, while Ida and Gwen became chambermaids, Ida for nearly sixty years. Teddy was for a time a chauffeur and driver, and Harry worked on the farm as a shepherd. Sammy followed his father as farm bailiff for a time, and Joan worked in the bar during the Second World War.

Hampson negotiated a limited ten-year lease on taking over in 1909. In view of what he knew of the financial problems of his two predecessors, this was wise. He had discovered, to use his own words, that:

'The first lessee, Mr Ward, lost a good many thousands in a few years. Miss Davies, after running the place many years died very poor. If she had not obtained a good price for the goodwill of the lease she would have been insolvent. She had been trading at a loss for some years when I took the business over.'

The actual amount Hampson paid Miss Davies for the lease was £2400, approximating to £270,000 today.

During his first five years at Vyrnwy, Hampson, who was clearly an efficient businessman, managed to make a profit. In 1913 the gross profit was £1552, leaving £1168 (about £128,000 today) after writing off depreciation of the lease, furniture, and other items.

His fortunes changed when the First World War started. By 1918 he was greatly concerned with the matter of who would take on the lease, which he was due to surrender the following year. It was important to him that the newcomers were financially strong enough to pay a good price for the goodwill of the business, the tenants' furnishings and fixtures, and several wooden buildings in the grounds. These buildings included the wooden house he had erected himself for his own use, one hundred yards from the Hotel beside the back drive, at a cost of £750. Now known as 'The Cottage', it is still the home of the general manager and his family.

Throughout 1918 Hampson was in constant correspondence with Mr W. Forrester Addie, the agent for the estate, and Lieutenant-Colonel J. R. Davidson, DSO, the Liverpool Corporation water engineer, on the subject of the new tenants. The Hotel was advertised in several journals and newspapers in early June 1918 in the following terms:

SPORTING ESTATE AND HOTEL, LAKE VYRNWY, NORTH WALES.

Owing to the Expiration of lease the first-class hotel belonging to the Liverpool Corporation at Lake Vyrnwy, with farm and extensive fishings, general shootings, and grouse moors, will be to LET from Lady Day, 1919. Tenders are invited for a Lease of the whole of the property or separate tenders for: (a) The Hotel, the farm, the fishing over the reservoir, tributary streams, and River Vyrnwy, and the general shootings; (b) the grouse moors.

THE HOTEL stands at a height of 1000 ft above sea level and commands a view of lake and mountain scenery of unsurpassed beauty. The Hotel contains

40 bedrooms, with private and public sitting rooms, bathrooms on all floors, a fine billiard room with lavatory attached and all modern conveniences. The building is lighted throughout by electricity. It is surrounded by attractive walks and drives through mountain and sylvan scenery. Connected with the Hotel are a garage, with separate stalls for five cars, stables, coach-house and the usual offices. Close to the main building there is a post and telegraph office with residence for the Postmaster. There are also conveniently situated five recently built workmen's cottages. A BUNGALOW of modern construction with eight bed-rooms may be included in the letting. Distance to the Hotel from Penybontfawr Station (Tanat Valley Ry.) eight miles, from Llanfyllin Station ten miles, from Chester 38 miles, and from Shrewsbury 30 miles. A FARM of about 500 acres, with necessary outbuildings, is Let with the Hotel.

THE FISHING includes extensive rights over Lake Vyrnwy and its tributary streams and over a length of the River Vyrnwy. The lake is the largest sheet of water in Wales, five miles long and twelve miles around on good level roads. Its high reputation for trout fishing is well known to anglers. There is a boat-house for sixteen boats. THE GENERAL SHOOTINGS embrace all the lands and woods owned by the Corporation in the Vyrnwy Catchment area of 18,000 acres (except the grouse moors). The grouse moors include four moors, having a total area of 6,000 acres well stocked and convenient of access.—For further particulars and orders to view apply to Messrs. ADDIE & SONS, Welshpool; or to the TOWN CLERK, Liverpool. Tenders must be sent in, in a sealed envelope endorsed

"Lake Vyrnwy Hotel", addressed to the Town Clerk, Municipal Buildings, Liverpool, by not later than noon on Monday, July 1st, 1918.

To some extent these advertisements were a waste of money, since, in the end, the lease was taken up by a syndicate of three members – Mr Caley, Mr Carkeet James and Major Lowndes – who had been expressing an interest in it well before any advertising was put in hand. A letter dated 2 March 1918 to Colonel Davidson from the Town Clerk of Liverpool reported an interview with Caley and James, in the latter's office in Broadway, which he considered 'very satisfactory'. In the letter the Town Clerk wrote:

'On the question of the form of the lease, I told him that the Corporation would prefer to have as lessees two or three responsible gentlemen who would be expected to give Bank references as to their responsibility, and that these gentlemen might sub-let the premises to a company or syndicate as they might desire, throughout being responsible for the payment of the rent, and the due fulfilment of the covenants of the lease. No objection was made to this suggestion.'

He also recorded that he had told James that the Corporation 'would require a minimum rent of £800 for the first two years, and subsequently a minimum rent of £1000 a year', not including the grouse moors.

Throughout the summer and autumn, negotiations continued, with the Caley, James and Lowndes syndicate the leading contender for the lease, but struggling hard to bring rents for the Hotel and the moors down to the lowest possible figures. A few other tenders were received following the advertising, but do not seem to have been serious.

As well as sustaining an offensive to lower rents, the syndicate worked hard to bring down the price of all the items they would have to buy from William Hampson. Caley made it his business to spend much of August and September at the Hotel, no doubt partly for the shooting as well as business. In a long letter to Colonel Davidson on 4 September 1918 Hampson gave vent to his feelings:

'Mr Caley has made himself a perfect nuisance in the Hotel, he has been there weeks prying into everything and upsetting everybody. He has complained to me of various things and I was inclined to blame Mr Bennett [the manager] but find there are two sides to consider.'

Matters had still not come to a satisfactory conclusion nearly two months later. Hampson was dismayed to hear that the syndicate's latest offer to the Corporation for the rent was well below the original figures demanded, being only £550 for two years and £750 for the remainder of the lease. With the possibility of this offer being refused, with all its consequences for him personally, he wrote again to Colonel Davidson on 25 October 1918, urging him to accept this offer even if it was less than the Corporation's original demand. Appalled by the thought that the syndicate might be turned down, leaving him unable to recover much of his own investment in the business, he explained that the new offer was in truth quite reasonable in view of the difficulty in finding tenants 'with sufficient capital who would be content to live in such an isolated place'. He finished his letter by saying: 'I cannot help thinking it will pay the Corporation to secure the Caley syndicate if possible, for another tenant at all suitable may take a long time to find'.

No doubt to Hampson's relief the long-drawn-out proceedings were at last concluded, and the trio took up the lease in the spring of 1919, allowing him reasonable terms for the goodwill, and for the tenants' fixtures and fittings. Even though the new lessees had negotiated what they no doubt considered were the best possible terms for gaining control of the Hotel and all its facilities, they were to find it as difficult as their predecessors to make a profit out of it. Some indication as to why comes from these notes written by George Westropp, who is a great-nephew of Major Lowndes:

'Major Lowndes had a joint reputation for eccentricity and generosity in our family. This combination and a background as a senior policeman in India rather than businessman goes some way towards explaining his lack of success as a hotelier.

My father recalled being collected with his mother in a pony and trap at Llanfyllin railway station and being driven the ten miles up to the Lake in the summer of 1923. His uncle, Johnnie Lowndes, greeted them at the Hotel and made the introductions to all the other guests over dinner. The whole Hotel was filled with immediate family, other free-loading relatives and friends of the syndicate. There was not a paying guest in the house and father remembered his two-week stay as a glorious house party.

Lowndes' passions were shooting and hunting. He considered trout thoroughly second rate compared with salmon fishing. Trolling a minnow was almost encouraged and Lowndes allowed his family to do so all over the Lake, although the rule was only between tower and dam.

There were trips over Bwlch-y-Groes to look at a partridge shoot that the syndicate had hired in the deep valley of Llanymawddwy and much time at the kennels of Johnnie's Lake Vyrnwy Foxhounds. Anybody who knows the area or anything about hunting will tell you that Vyrnwy is not the place to hunt foxes on horseback. But, Lowndes did so and financed the whole enterprise out of the syndicate's dwindling coffers.

Those few guests who did pay, experienced an unusual diet. Johnnie had read in *The Times* that kippers were good for the brain and full of protein. He immediately sent away for a barrel of them. For a week after, there were kippers for breakfast, lunch, tea, and dinner until the residents mutinied. It did them no good. Kippers stayed on the menu until the barrel was empty. One wonders how many returned to the Hotel; regular clientele were the bread and butter of Vyrnwy as a business.

While young, I discovered a number of staff who had worked for the Major and everybody enthused over his kindness and generosity. Sick children from the village, I learned, had been sent all the way to specialists in London for treatment out of his own pocket. And 'Mervyn Davies the Tower' took care of a fine clock presented by Johnnie to the British Legion. As a very small boy, I was taken to see Johnnie in an old people's nursing home near Simonsbath, Exmoor, by my uncle Colonel Monty Westropp and my father. I recognised that he was rather odd. "Poor Johnnie", my father explained, "kindest man I ever met but quite, quite hopeless with money."'

In 1925, the syndicate decided that it was time to give up the pleasant but costly trade of hotel keeping, and the lease was assigned to the Walkers, a young, recently retired Lieutenant RN and his wife, Belinda. On taking over in 1926 they negotiated a new twenty-one-year lease, due to expire in 1947. Baldwin Walker was the son of a retired Rear-Admiral, also a baronet, who was commissioner, or land agent, to the Duke of

Northumberland. Belinda had been a Barnett, one of a well-known Northumberland family, before her first marriage to a naval officer called Ball. It was involvement in her divorce from Ball that caused Baldwin Walker to resign from the Royal Navy; in those days even the remotest connection with a divorce case was social and professional death in service circles.

Before coming to Lake Vyrnwy, the Walkers had lived in the village of Cleobury Mortimer in Shropshire. With them came a young man called Billy Thomas, whose father owned a shop in that village, and a farm worker's daughter named Alice Turner. Both remained involved in the Hotel for many years. Billy married Ida Hill, and their son John, born in 1930, also worked in it for a long time before taking on the shop at Dafarn Newydd. Alice married Walter Carpenter, member of a local family, and had a large family. She was still doing part-time work in the Hotel over fifty years after coming to the valley.

Sadly, Baldwin Walker contracted tuberculosis soon after arriving at Vyrnwy, and died in 1927. He was reported to have been one of the few people ever able to keep his wife under control. After his death Belinda took full charge of the Hotel, and ran it with considerable flair and success. Being a strong character, without too much sympathy for other people's feelings, she rarely failed to get her own way in any business she undertook. Although not particularly good looking, and careless of her appearance, she was a vibrant personality, capable of being charming and kind as well as hard and demanding. One man who found her highly attractive was a serving Squadron-Leader, later Wing-Commander, in the RAF called Graham Martin, who began to court her soon after Walker's death. He pressed his suit by often flying over the Hotel, and once or twice dropping letters for her from the air. In due course they were married, and had one son. This brought Belinda's total of children to four, since she already had a daughter by Ball, and two sons by Walker. To add to the family there was Martin's son by his first wife, named John.

John Martin, a Lieutenant Colonel retired from long service with the 10th Gurkha Rifles, had vivid memories of Lake Vyrnwy in the 1930s. The first was not a happy one. Aged four, he had his first meeting with his new stepmother. When she announced that she was now his mummy, was to be called mummy, and that he was to forget his other mummy and never talk about her again, he remembers running from the room shouting 'I hate you! I hate you!' This was probably in his favour in the long run, since he recalls that she treated people better who stood up to her. Those who did not could be trampled upon if necessary.

His father was a charming, easy-going Irishman with an altogether different character. He loved flying, motor-racing, shooting, and fishing and had little aptitude for business. To his son he was not only a kind father but a good friend, who took a delight in passing on his own knowledge of field sports. On 20 September 1937 Graham's game-book proudly records: 'Took John out with his gun for the first time.' The two of them shot a brace of grouse, a duck, and a rabbit.

Before the Second World War most guests changed into dinner jackets and long evening dresses for dinner. Those who did not could be made to feel uncomfortable. A permanent resident in the Hotel for some years was Lieutenant-Colonel the Hon. Robert Lygon, late of the Grenadier Guards, whose beady eye was quickly turned on anyone he considered unsuitably dressed.

Perhaps young John Martin's happiest times were spent with members of the staff. John Hill taught him how to look after a pony, and how to clean his tack properly, as well as passing on much country lore. Mrs Hill, who was always dressed in Victorian style with a cameo brooch at the throat of her high black collar, was unfailingly kind to him when he visited her house. He remembers all the other members of the family with great affection as well. Another good friend was chauffeur Billy Thomas, with whom he often travelled in one of the two cars kept at the Hotel, the Rolls-Royce, or the big, wooden-bodied

Ford shooting-brake. Among the indoor staff, Mary Morris, the chambermaid, was a great favourite.

Another person to remember well the 1930s was Mrs Doris Moss, in those days Miss Grey, usually known as Dolly, who worked in the Hotel as secretary and receptionist. She recorded some interesting recollections of the times:

'When I first arrived at Lake Vyrnwy, the Hotel was very different structurally. The present pantry was the housekeeper's room, "the piggery", where the housekeeper, the receptionist and the "chicken lady" ate and sat, sometimes being invaded by family and regular visitors at busy times. The refrigerator was downstairs, one very large one with different compartments for freshwater fish, sea fish, meat, etc. at different temperatures. The present dining room was divided, there being the steward's room at one end and the part nearest the office was the bar. The present bar was the large dining room and the present drawing room was the small dining room. The drawing room was on the first floor where No. I now is.

The kitchen had an old-fashioned coal-fired range and there was an old-fashioned bread oven in the back yard where part of The Tavern now is. The kitchen boy had to collect wood and light the fire in the oven as required. We baked all our own bread.

We were very much more self-supporting. We had our own cows and only had to buy milk and cream when the Hotel was full. We also had our own sheep and our own free-range chickens. Eggs had to be bought in the high season only. We also put down eggs during the winter for use for cooking in the summer. We also killed our own fowl. We usually had sex-linked cockerels for table birds. We had sows and a boar. The piglets were sold about six weeks old. This was an amusing business as Stanley Davies from Llanfyllin, a brother of the late Rt Hon. Clement Davies, M.P., would come and bargain with John Hill our farm bailiff and then come to the office where the deal was made and Stanley Davies departed with the piglets – and a bottle of whisky.

Dry goods came once a month from Hudson Bros, London, meat from Brodricks, Liverpool, but home-killed meat from Embrey at Nesscliffe. Butter came from Wathes Bros, a Shropshire firm. Mac-Fisheries supplied a certain amount of fish. Their representative called one day during the summer to offer us frozen pheasants – quite regardless of the fact that we sold them fresh pheasants after every syndicate shoot.

One year we had let a certain part of the pheasant shoot to two old gentlemen and they had come up in August to see how the birds were coming on. One evening at dinner time a guest came to inform us that his son had gone out rabbit shooting, without permission, and had not returned. A search party was just being organised when he returned carrying two pheasant chicks he had shot on the rearing field. Naturally, the two old gentlemen saw the boy arrive and things became awkward. Eventually one of the old gentlemen demanded compensation from the boy's father and when it was forthcoming the other gentlemen insisted it should be given to the church offertory. The guest and his son left the next day.

In August there was usually an evening picnic at the top end of the Lake for the younger and more adventurous guests, who would sometimes help to remove the chub from the shallow water by various means – kicking, spearing, shooting or tickling. Those picnics were quite a hazard and it seemed that every fly, midge and mosquito in the neighbourhood joined in, and even a smudge fire did not improve the situation.

There were also Treasure Hunts and also occasionally on moonlight nights drives round the Lake in open cars shooting at rabbits – the gun sitting on the bonnet. During the summer, evening dress was worn every night except Sunday and there was often dancing to gramophone records after dinner.

At the beginning of July each year Liverpool Corporation members descended in strength. The Lord Mayor had his footmen in attendance and he wore his Mayoral Chain for their special dinner. They had the small dining room (as it then was) at their disposal and the upstairs drawing room as a sitting room. On one occasion they had just left after tea in the drawing room when one or two regular visitors wanted tea, so it was suggested they should go up to the drawing room to get away from the crowd. About ten minutes later a rather shaken guest came down to say that part of the ceiling had fallen on them.

This also happened once in the present bar on Good Friday morning. A very upset barman came to the office saying that a large lump of ceiling just by the fireplace had fallen missing him by inches. Humphrey Howard came to the rescue.

Every year in September there was the Sheep Sale. Liverpool Corporation sold a large number of sheep and we sold some of ours. The sale was held in the field above the

Hotel and meals were served in the staff room, steward's room, and the dining room most of the day. Guests were warned about this but many enjoyed the whole show. The numbers of sellers, shepherds, etc., that came for a meal, to be put down to Mr Stanley Davies' account, was quite surprising, but the account was never queried.

In the winter of 1937 we had the experience of being snowed up. We were lucky that it happened on a Saturday night, when we had about a dozen guests in the Hotel, as we had collected our stores and fresh vegetables on Friday. The snow started about 10pm and there was about an inch of snow by 11pm. During the night the wind rose and there was quite a blizzard. The snow was up to the glass on the front door by morning and many trees were down all round the Lake and also patches of several hundred had been toppled. The telephone wires were down and the roads were blocked.

The visitors and staff passed the time in the afternoons tobogganing down from the front drive over the field to the road on old tea trays. It was several days before the roads were cleared for traffic to get through with supplies and the village was getting short of bread and flour.

One year the British Waterways Association decided to have their Annual General Meeting at Lake Vyrnwy, which involved our having to supply lunch and tea for 350. It was decided that a marquee would be put up on the tennis court. As far as I remember they had hot soup but otherwise it was a cold meal. We had to hire waitresses and a certain amount of crockery but we decided to order four hundred new coffee cups from Wedgwood & Co., Stoke-on-Trent. These went missing on the railway and arrived the evening before the great day. As you can imagine the telephone lines were red hot.

For some time we used to do meals for coach parties, which had to be booked in advance. It could be frustrating as whatever menus were suggested they always wanted tomato soup and roast chicken.

On one occasion a high tea had been arranged for a party walking over from Arran Mawddwy to arrive about 5pm. It was nearly seven o'clock when the phone rang and we were informed they had lost one of the party but most of them would be arriving. This turned out to be a tragedy as one boy had strayed and fallen over a ledge and had been killed. The press got hold of the story and the telephone rang incessantly. We eventually persuaded everyone that they would get more information from Dinas Mawddwy as the search party had set out from there. In the end we rang the exchange and said we would not accept any more calls until the morning.'

Humphrey Howard, the Corporation's resident agent on the estate, came to the rescue on many other occasions as well and Belinda took care to maintain an excellent working relationship with him.

Although the storm-clouds were gathering over Europe during the second half of the 1930s, and thoughtful people were increasingly worried about the resurgence of a belligerent Germany ruled by Adolf Hitler, life was pleasant for people who had the wherewithal to stay at Lake Vyrnwy. Under Belinda's efficient management, the Hotel was well run and adequately prosperous, while Graham Martin's knowledge of field sports ensured that the sporting side flourished. For a short period after the declaration of war with Germany on 3 September 1939

1. The north face of the dam at Vyrnwy under construction.
2. The dam and the valley in 1888 before submersion.

3. The Powis Arms Hotel in old Llanwddyn village with the church of St. John in the background.

4. A villager ferrying his last possessions across the Lake in 1888.

5.   The Hotel in about 1893.

6.   Looking down to the Lake from the hill behind the Hotel c1900.

7. The Hotel in the days of the proprietor Miss Davies, standing in the foreground, in c1900.

8. Llwynrhiw Bay, early 1900s – one of the paintings commissioned by the Liverpool Corporation for a series of postcards of the Lake.

9. & 10. Both photographs show the shooting party at the Hotel in 1901 of George Guyse Barker (*fourth from the right on the lower photograph*). They were presented to the Hotel by Mr Barker's son Brigadier Charles N. Barker, M.C.

No.1. Lake Vyrnwy Hotel.

11. The Hotel after the 1905 addition.

12. The visit in 1910 by the Prince of Wales (later George V) who is standing in the doorway of the Hotel.

Lake Vyrnwy Hotel. Visit of King George (then Prince of Wales) March 1910.

13. Major Lowndes with his hounds and Miss Ruby Hill, his whipper-in, in the field above the Hotel in April 1923.

14. An aerial view of the Hotel taken by Squadron-Leader Graham Martin on 26th March 1928, at the time he was courting his future wife, Belinda.

15. Billy Thomas in his chauffeur's cap standing beside the Martin's Rolls-Royce in 1939. Don the Spaniel enjoys a perch on the running-board.

16. Guests and boatmen after the annual Boatmen's Fishing Competition in the late 1930s – taken outside the main entrance of the Hotel. *Back Row*: Mr Jack Roberts, A. N. Other, Mr Larman, Mr King, Captain Tanner, Mr Humphrey Howard, Mrs M. Martin, Commander Taylor and Mr Graham Martin. *Middle Row*: Mr Cadwallader Williams, Edwin Humphries, 'Sim' Carpenter, Walter Carpenter, Albert Carpenter and George Morris. *Front Row*: 'Willy' Edwards, Felix Evans, Bernard Hughes, Owen Thomas, 'Willy' Morris, 'Sim' Carpenter Jnr, 'Joey' Morris, Harry Jones, Joe Morris and Bob Roberts.

there was little change in the way of life in rural areas like the Vyrnwy valley. The pinch was first felt when men started to be called away to serve in the armed forces, or to do some form of civilian work devoted to the war effort. Graham Martin was soon back in RAF uniform, while Billy Thomas was directed to factory work near Wolverhampton. Many Corporation workers were similarly called up, with only a proportion given reserved occupation status in order to keep the estate going. Those that remained at home were employed in forestry and farming; there was no labour available for luxuries like shooting and fishing. Only a few elderly men past retirement age were available to act as occasional boatmen on the Lake, while the switch of all the gamekeepers to other work meant that only rough shooting could take place. Yet, in spite of many difficulties, the Hotel itself flourished during the war, as will unfold in the next chapter.

CHAPTER FIVE

War and Peace: 1940–2018

IN direct contrast to William Hampson's experience during the First World War, the Second was for Belinda Martin the busiest and most profitable period in her long tenancy of the Hotel. For some five years, hardly a night passed without every bed in the place being full, and sometimes unusual rooms were used to provide extra accommodation. On a visit to the Hotel in the 1970s, the elderly Belinda was walking along the first-floor corridor when she passed the door of the ladies' lavatory, at the time situated near the top of the back stairs. 'Often shoved a couple of extra beds in there in the war,' she announced. During the war the vicar moved out of the large stone-built vicarage, which then stood on the site of the present, much smaller, house; it was later pulled down because of dry rot. Quick to spot an opportunity, Belinda contrived to obtain use of it as an annexe to the Hotel.

A remarkable range of people occupied the Hotel in the war years. A royal family must head the list. After the occupation of their country by the Japanese in 1942, King Prajadhipok of Siam (present-day Thailand) with his Queen, and the Crown Prince with his wife and baby, were given refuge in Britain. To provide them with a safe place to stay, Lake Vyrnwy was chosen, and they made the Hotel their home for over two years. They occupied five of the best rooms on the first floor overlooking the Lake, and were looked after devotedly by Ida Thomas and her sister Gwen, who remembered them with great affection.

Under a scheme instigated by Lord Nuffield, the car manufacturer, and bearing his name, Lake Vyrnwy became an official leave centre for officers of the armed forces. Among the many who took advantage of the scheme, the majority were airmen, including a high proportion of Polish pilots. A number of Dutch officers from the Netherlands army contingent based around Wolverhampton also frequented the Hotel. Belinda enjoyed the company of the Poles, reputedly to quite an extent in one or two cases, but that may have been just gossip. Other servicemen to come on leave included those who did so under their own private arrangements, using petrol coupons, which were allowed in small quantities for this purpose. Among this group were Wing Commander James (Jamie) Moir, AFC, with his wife, Ruth, and two sons, who always tried to spend his spells of leave at Vyrnwy.

Towards the end of the war, the Hotel was even home to a few officers who were in the area on duty. After the successful breaching of the Möhne dam in Germany by the 'Dambusters' in 1943, it was feared that the Luftwaffe might attempt a retaliatory attack on some major dam in Britain. A troop of anti-aircraft guns was therefore sent to Vyrnwy, and took up positions to protect the dam. The officers were accommodated in the Hotel, while the soldiers used a large hut erected near the estate offices at the south end of the dam. This hut was dismantled after the war and re-erected opposite the side door of the Hotel on the site of the erstwhile post office. Here it was used for many years as a games room and store, or as a rod room.

The list of war-time occupants also included a group of the masters and boys of a small preparatory school, evacuated from a dangerous home in the south of England. A large number of rooms on the top floor of the Hotel were allotted to the school, as well as William Hampson's Cottage in the grounds,

Even with all these varied people staying in the Hotel, there was always room for ordinary civilian visitors to be squeezed in wherever possible. Members of the Liverpool City Council, and officials of the Corporation, continued to make their regular visits: there was every temptation to do so whenever possible, since peaceful nights and access to farm produce were preferable to bombs on the city and rationing.

The negligible risk of bombing, added to the presence of a lot of young officers enjoying a spell of rest and tranquility, produced a happy atmosphere in the Hotel. Such discomforts as there were could easily be ignored by people inured to far worse conditions elsewhere in war-time Britain, or overseas in theatres of action. Most evenings there was dancing in the hall to a radiogram. Ruth Moir remembers periods of leave during the war as particularly enjoyable, though there was one aspect that she and Jamie found an embarrassment.

Strict food-rationing made hotel catering difficult for everyone, especially in the towns. In rural areas like Montgomeryshire, it was made easier by access to such treasures as eggs, butter, and bacon purchased from farms, which in those days almost invariably provided such items for themselves. Billy Thomas was often on the road to farms all over the countryside to pick up quantities of such goods. The trouble was that the distribution of them to the Hotel residents was not entirely fair. Belinda organised the dining room in such a way that she sat at a large table for up to sixteen people, situated in the far side of the central pillar, which still divides the room more or less into two parts. At this table sat her favoured young airmen, and special friends such as the Moirs, who had known the Martins for many years, going back to the time when Jamie and Graham had served in the same squadron in the RAF in the early 1930s. While the guests in the large end of the dining room made do with largely rationed food, the quality of that served at Belinda's private table was almost up to pre-war standards. Knowing what was being doled out to most of their fellow guests made the Moirs feel awkward about eating their own sumptuous meals.

To keep the Hotel running satisfactorily, a supply of petrol was essential, not only for Billy's foraging expeditions to farms, but for meeting guests from, and delivering them to, various railway stations and pick-up points. To obtain the necessary quantities of strictly rationed fuel, Belinda used all her wiles and guile, playing the importance of the leave centre as her trump card in her legal search for extra petrol coupons. Having little time for regulations or red tape, she was not averse to picking them up in the black market as well. Using every possible means she managed to keep the wheels of the Hotel vehicles rolling throughout the war.

The vehicle most used was the Ford V8 shooting-brake, with its body-work made of wood, as was the fashion in those days. There were two main collecting-cum-delivery points for guests: Llanfyllin railway station, and a halt at Bryngwyn, two miles east on the line to Oswestry. This, however, was not used for meeting trains, but as a point to collect people coming from Oswestry by taxi. Its significance lay in the fact that it was just ten miles from the town, and therefore on the extreme limit of the distance that war-time regulations allowed a taxi to travel on any one journey. Bryngwyn halt was demolished when the railway line to Llanfyllin was closed in the 1960s.

As the war neared its close in 1945, a small incident occurred that was to have quite an effect on the future of the Hotel. The Lord Mayor of Liverpool and one of his senior colleagues came to Vyrnwy for an important meeting with Humphrey Howard. They were not given good rooms, but put into two singles on the first floor at the back, directly over the hall, where next morning at 2am a cheerful, noisy party was still in progress. The Lord Mayor could not get to sleep. Accompanied by his colleague, both in pyjamas and dressing gowns, he appeared on the stairs and ordered the party to be brought to an end, and the noisy members of it, mainly airmen, to go to bed. 'Don't you know there's a war on,' shouted one very large young pilot, who promptly ran up the stairs and picked the Lord Mayor up bodily. Others dealt similarly with his partner, and the two protesting dignitaries were carried to their rooms, told to shut up, and dumped on their beds. The party was then resumed. Had Belinda been present she would undoubtedly have stopped the proceedings at an early stage: though prepared to treat the Lord Mayor in a fairly casual fashion, she would have realised that this was going a little too far.

In May 1945, VE Day was celebrated with the relief and abandon seen in the rejoicing all over Britain. When VJ Day came in August, Ruth Moir happened to be staying in the Hotel with her two sons. On hearing of the Japanese surrender, Belinda at once announced that everyone due to leave that day must stay for a party that night. When it was pointed out that nearly all the guests she referred to were about to depart, with a whole mass of new ones coming in to take their places, she remained unmoved. Declaring that this was of no importance, she ordered mattresses to be put on the floors of all the larger rooms, and announced that everyone could double up for such hours of the night that would remain after the party. Ruth and her two sons found themselves in Room 39, as three out of a total of eight occupants. Nobody seemed to mind, or, if they did, they knew it was no use complaining.

Belinda's twenty-one-year lease was due to end in the spring of 1947. Assuming that there would be no difficulty in renewing it, she applied to the Corporation to do so, but to her amazement, and fury, her application was refused. Undoubtedly the recent treatment of the Lord Mayor had done little to help her cause. It is likely that various officials from Liverpool had received more cavalier treatment than they felt their position deserved during war-time visits, even if not quite so extreme as that meted out to the Lord Mayor. All this had built up a determination at city headquarters to find a new tenant for the Hotel. This was a problem for Belinda that not even Humphrey Howard was able to solve for her.

In 1946, Jamie Moir ended his service in the RAF, and

determined to take up farming. Having been brought up and worked on his father's large farm in New Zealand, before coming to Britain to join the RAF in the 1920s, he had a good knowledge of farming practice, especially with livestock. They had grown very fond of the Vyrnwy area during many visits to the Hotel, and he and Ruth came to stay there as a base from which to start searching for a farm in the neighbourhood. On discovering that Belinda's application for renewal had been turned down, and that tenders were being sought from new potential tenants, they decided to make an offer themselves. The 435-acre Hotel farm would give Jamie his chance to indulge his interest in farming, while Ruth found the prospect of helping to run the Hotel more attractive than that of being purely a farmer's wife.

The closing date for tenders was 14 November 1946, and five days later the Town Clerk listed the particulars of six people who had put in serious offers. Of these, the Moirs and three others were asked to come to Liverpool on 25 November to be interviewed by the Water Committee, who decided that of the four they were the ones to be granted the lease, even though their offer was not the highest.

Having successfully achieved their aim of becoming lessees, the Moirs soon discovered that their troubles were only just beginning. When she learnt that she was to lose her lease, Belinda lost interest in the business. She spent several months of 1946 touring Africa with some of her Polish friends, leaving Graham Martin to supervise the Hotel in a rather luke-warm fashion. Following the hectic years of the war, when little maintenance could be carried out, this period of inattention by the proprietors saw the condition of the Hotel, the farm, and the grounds sink into a state of general dilapidation. This was compounded by the difficulty of agreeing with Belinda a realistic figure to be paid for the contents of the Hotel, the goodwill, and the other assets of the business. And to make matters even worse, the early months of 1947, while all this was being sorted out, saw the longest and coldest winter of the century enfold the country in a deep blanket of snow and ice. For some weeks, no motor vehicles could get through to the valley, and supplies for Llanwddyn and the Hotel came on horse-drawn sledges, or in panniers on the back of a horse. Any person needing to travel to or from the area had to walk much of the way to Llanfyllin along a narrow track between high banks of snow.

Eventually, more or less satisfactory terms were arranged with Belinda, who is remembered departing from the Hotel on a horse-drawn sledge, accompanied by the man from Jackson Stopps and Staff, who had been sent to value the stock and contents, perched on the back, looking thoroughly incongruous in a bowler hat. The Moirs moved in just as the thaw began in early April, to spend their first night in the Hotel in a leaking bedroom, where they were forced to move buckets around at frequent intervals to catch drops from the ceiling. Because of the appalling state of the building, made worse by the ravages of the winter, the Corporation eventually agreed to spend over two thousand pounds – about £75,000 today – in redecorating it and repairing the roof. The decision to do this, and so give the Moirs a reasonable start, was largely due to the intercession of Humphrey Howard, who was to prove himself as good an ally to them as he had been to their predecessors.

A great strength of Lake Vyrnwy Hotel has always been the loyalty and efficiency of its long serving staff. The Moirs were fortunate to take on many key employees who had spent most of their lives working there. Having known the Hotel well as guests, they had the advantage of knowing the majority of their new staff quite well already. Members of the Hill family and their dependants were strongly represented. John, son of Billy and Ida Thomas, had joined his parents in the Hotel, and in 1949 was put in charge of the taproom at the young age of 19. He was to fill this position with great efficiency for the next twenty-five years. Another family with several members involved were the

Morrises. Mary and her niece Annie were chambermaids, and Mary's brother Joey was a regular boatman.

The weak link in the employment chain was in the kitchen. The practice was to hire chefs for 'the season', which meant the period from Easter each year to November. In 1947 a pleasant Swiss man was taken on, but proved an indifferent cook. He returned in 1948, but the food he produced was so bad that Ruth Moir suggested he should be removed. Instead, she promoted an Italian prisoner-of-war, who had been employed as a kitchen porter, to take his place. Under her supervision, Vittorio Cottiga, who had a natural flair for cooking, blossomed into an excellent chef. When he eventually left, Ruth, who had done some courses at the Cordon Bleu school, took charge of the kitchen herself. Over the years, a stream of girls came to help her and learn from her. These were mainly daughters and relations of the Moirs' personal friends, or of regular Hotel guests. The style of cooking she developed was based on relatively simple, even homely, recipes, but adjusted for large numbers. Excellent soups, including proper homemade consommé, pâtés, game, roasts, and simple puddings were the mainstay of menus, which were greatly appreciated by the type of guests who enjoyed similar food in their own homes. Those who were out each day on the Lake fishing, or some other activity, particularly appreciated the generous breakfasts and substantial packed lunches.

On taking over the Hotel farm, Jamie Moir was faced with the prospect of a difficult period of reorganisation before it could run again to his satisfaction. During the war, fences and gates had fallen into disrepair, and required a great deal of work to put right. Fortunately, the Corporation helped with this to some extent. The terrible winter of 1947 had wreaked havoc among the sheep flocks in the district, with the carcasses of dead sheep lying everywhere as the snows finally melted. Such animals as were left alive were in a poor state, while the lambs born to the few ewes that survived were weak and sickly, an easy prey to the numerous and hungry foxes that proliferated at the time. Eventually the Hotel flock was built up again to a strength of four hundred breeding ewes, whose lambs were the most sought after of all those sold each September at the sales held in the field to the north of the Hotel, at the top of the rise beyond The Tavern.

The Hotel farm's 435 acres were divided into two parts: 89 acres of low-ground land, and 346 acres of sheep-walk. For a few years, some oats were grown each summer on the low-ground. In the autumn, a threshing machine would trundle up to the Hotel to be set up at the end of the farm buildings below the doors of what was then the granary. The threshed corn was kept for feeding stock, and the straw stacked to be cut up as chaff for the same purpose in the winter.

As the years passed the labour force on the farm was reduced by economic pressure. The first to go was Sammy Hill, who had followed his father John as bailiff. By the end of the 1950s, Jamie was working the farm almost single-handedly, with only occasional help, as well as running the Hotel. Even his remarkable constitution could not stand the pace forever, and he decided to give up the tenancy of most of the land in 1961. However, he retained some fifteen acres close to the Hotel on which to keep two or three Jersey cows to provide milk for the Hotel. These he milked himself every day, thus keeping some contact with the farming that was his first love.

During the Moirs' years the Hotel was run with meticulous efficiency, and kept spotlessly clean throughout. The polished furniture in the public rooms and the top of the residents' bar always gleamed. The relatively formal way in which the daily routine was conducted suited most of the guests, many of whom had service backgrounds like the proprietors themselves. They expected to have dinner at a set time, and to dress tidily for it. Such people as did not enjoy the atmosphere did not stay long, often having been made aware that they were not particularly welcome. For the important regular guests, nothing was ever too much trouble, and many of them came once or twice a year for quite long stays.

As the year 1968 approached, so did the end of the twenty-one-year lease granted to the Moirs in 1947. They decided to apply for an extension of five years, to run from 1968 to 1973. The Liverpool Corporation was quite agreeable to this, but wished to decide on a new rent at the start of the extended period. They commissioned Harper Webb and Co., a Chester firm of chartered surveyors, to inspect the Hotel and make a recommendation as to what the annual rent should be. Two paragraphs from their report give a good insight into the Moirs' guardianship of the Hotel:

'Although Mr Moir had apparently no experience of the hotel trade prior to his taking occupation of the Lake Vyrnwy Hotel in 1947, from our comparatively brief association with him on the occasion of our inspection of the property we formed the opinion that he has natural aptitude as a proprietor and we were very favourably impressed by what we saw of the manner in which the establishment is being run. Due to the great difficulty in obtaining regular staff both he and his wife are, we understand, regularly engaged in providing services well beyond the scope of what we would expect from the proprietors of a hotel of this size, such as cultivation and maintenance of the gardens and grounds and all of the cooking. There is no doubt that they display great industry and resource in not only running the business but also maintaining the property in a manner that exceeds their strict obligations under the lease.

In the circumstances we find it difficult to quote a hard and fast figure as our opinion of the rental value of this property in the open market on the terms quoted to us, on which an extension of the present lease would be granted for a further five years. In fact, on the basis of the figures shown in the accounts we examined, we think that the Corporation would be hard put to find another tenant able and willing to carry on the established business in place of the present lessee who, so he informs us, is able to supplement his return by a private income.'

Based on the Harper Webb recommendations, the rent offered by the Moirs was accepted, and their lease was renewed for five years. As the 1960s ended, age began to take its toll on some long-serving members of the staff. Due to heart trouble, Billy Thomas was forced to work for only a few hours a day, with a fraction of his former energy. Selwyn Jones was recruited to help him, and gradually took over the job of hotel porter from him. Mary Morris retired from being a full-time chambermaid, though she was allowed to keep a room in the Hotel and lived there until her death at the age of eighty. She had worked there all her life, from the age of fifteen, when she started as the staff maid. A year or two later, Ida Thomas also retired, after over fifty years of good service. Not only were members of the staff feeling the weight of the passing years, but even Jamie Moir's stamina was being taxed as he approached his seventieth birthday, leading him to make the decision to retire in 1972.

This is the stage at which I personally enter the story of the Hotel. While Jamie was anxious to retire, Ruth, some fourteen years his junior, wished to carry on with the business. To do so she needed a partner, to look after the numerous jobs that had been her husband's responsibility, and in particular to run the sporting estate. One attempt to set up such a partnership had fallen through shortly before I came to stay at Vyrnwy in May 1972, having finished twenty-six years in the regular army the previous month. I was combining a stay at the Hotel, with my wife Shirley and my father, with a visit to a firm in Birmingham where I had been offered the possibility of a job. Arriving at the head office of the firm I found that the job had been provisionally offered to someone else already. However, knowing of Ruth's search for a partner I wondered whether to suggest myself as a candidate. After a day of fishing and discussion on the Lake with my wife and father I decided to do so. My offer was accepted, a partnership agreement was drawn up, a new twenty-one-year lease was negotiated, and on 1 November 1972 Ruth and I started in business together.

Apart from one or two bumps in the early years, the course of our partnership ran remarkably smoothly. This was mainly due to a clear definition of responsibilities between us, and an avoidance on both sides of interference in the other's domain. Even if, looking back over the fourteen-plus years we worked together, there were things I now think we could have done better, I am grateful that such harmony prevailed between us. I gather that small business partnerships are not often so successful in this direction, and I must pay full tribute to Ruth for being such a splendid colleague to work with, who so consistently maintained the highest standards in her department.

I am not going to say much more about the years 1972 to 1986. In other chapters there is mention of the improvements we made to the buildings, and of the build-up of the pheasant shoot. However, I would like to quote extracts from two books that gave us pleasure in our last full year in business together. *The Good Food Guide* in 1986 made these comments:

'There are few concessions to modernity at Mrs Moir's shooting-lodge above the Lake, which she has run since 1947. Good-value menus include home-made soups, mixed fish quiche, cold meats, traditional roasts, salads, marvellous chutneys and good old-style bread-and-butter pudding. Coffee is served in the sumptuous lounge. Game is shot on the estate ... The non-vintage and inexpensive wine list includes a few bargains, such as St Julien '80, from the Barton stable, at £7.50.'

Somewhat to our surprise, but definitely to our delight, *The Good Hotel Guide* gave us one of its ten César Awards for 1986. These awards, it explains, 'are given for different sorts of excellence among hotels in Britain and Ireland'. Our citation read as follows:

'For preserving traditional values in a sporting hotel. Colonel Sir John Baynes and Mrs Moir know what they are about. They make no concessions to any modern image, but maintain with conspicuous success the virtues of a comfortable old-fashioned sporting hotel.'

When the Lake Vyrnwy estate was about to be passed from the Liverpool Corporation to the Severn Trent Water Authority (STWA) in 1973, I had written to the Corporation offering to purchase the freehold of the Hotel and the sporting rights. This followed an unofficial enquiry among the tenants as to which of them might be interested in buying their freeholds. In the end the decision was made at headquarters in Liverpool that no sales would be made, and when the newly established STWA assumed control on 1 April 1974 it decided to carry on the Corporation policy of retaining all property on the watershed of the Lake in its own hands.

Then, in 1984, we heard that the STWA might change its mind, and that the offers of tenants to buy their freeholds might be given consideration. Ruth and I decided to test the matter out, and wrote to say that we wished to buy the Hotel and its thirty-six acres of grounds. Receiving a positive response, we set about negotiating terms and conditions of purchase, and in 1985 became the freeholders of the property. Early the following year we came to a decision to end our partnership, as both of us wanted to climb off what might be called the 'tread-mill' of hotel-keeping to pursue other interests.

The sale of the Hotel was put in the hands of Robert Barry and Co. of Cirencester. The partner in charge of negotiations was Mr Hugh Guillebaud. During the summer of 1986 some thirty potential buyers came to look over the Hotel and the grounds. When tenders were called for in September there were nine serious offers. Of these, that of Mr Jim Bisiker was accepted. It was arranged that the actual hand-over of the Hotel would take place on 1 February 1987. All members of the staff were told that they would be taken on by the new owners from that date if they wished to continue working for them. During the final weekend of the old regime, Iain Gregory, who had run the residents' bar with great efficiency since 1980, unfortunately suffered a collapsed lung and had to be rushed into hospital. Due to his ill-health he and his wife, Jeannie, who had been such an excellent secretary and receptionist in the Hotel during the same period, were the only members of the staff unable to carry on under the new management.

Mr Jim Bisiker formed the company called Marketglen to run the business for him. I remained in partnership with the company with the primary task of showing Brian Bisiker, who was given charge of the sporting side under the auspices of the newly created Vyrnwy Sporting Company, all that I could about this vital aspect of the Hotel's affairs. This happy relationship lasted for many years.

An extensive programme of work was put in hand to restore and refurbish the ground-floor rooms in the Hotel, and to modernise the bedrooms upstairs in order to provide thirty exclusively en-suite bedrooms. This was a natural continuation of the process, mentioned in Chapter 3, whereby each generation has found it necessary to alter and update the buildings in some way. The quality of the work done was of a very high order, and the main public rooms were redecorated with care to make them more comfortable without destroying their traditional charm. This led to the Hotel becoming one of the pre-eminent country house hotels in Wales and resulted in Brian Bisiker being featured on the front cover of the *Caterer and Hotelkeeper* magazine (now *The Caterer*), a significant accolade at the time.

Naturally enough, the prospect of change gave rise to some misgivings among the regular visitors who knew and loved the Hotel in its previous state. Although there were some who ceased to come to it, most of the old regular guests renewed their patronage, and still return at their accustomed times to pursue their special interests, not least the co-author of this book George Westropp and his family. Among these well-established supporters were some intrepid motorcyclists, a group of whom were first brought to Vyrnwy in 1972 by Mr Peter Sheen, who became Director-General of the British Motorcycle Industry Association. Calling themselves 'The Club', these twenty or more senior executives from the motor industry should not be thought of as elderly 'Hell's Angels', but properly regarded as responsible citizens, in spite of their somewhat bizarre outfits when setting out on their motorcycle tours of the Welsh countryside.

The Club's twenty-first anniversary had previously been celebrated in 1984 at the Hotel, and guest of honour was the famous John Surtees, renowned as having been world racing champion on both two and four wheels. Due to the fact that the members enjoyed the Hotel's excellent house Bordeaux, Tanner's claret, and on one occasion drank the cellar dry of it, the name of their club was eventually changed to the 'Tanners Club'. In honour of this they were all invited to an excellent dinner in 1991 in the head office, and main cellars, of Tanners Wines in Shrewsbury. Since much of the Hotel's wine had been provided by this remarkable private firm of wine merchants for a century, this was a most appropriate occasion.

As well as retaining the support of the majority of its long-standing patrons, the Hotel was and has remained successful in attracting many new visitors. Those of us who have known Lake Vyrnwy over a long stretch of time, and regard it as a very special place, have reason to be grateful for the way in which the Bisiker family and those who work for them have been able to modernise the Hotel, without losing its charm.

Such was the success of the hotel business, it was decided to build an extension encompassing eight new large and luxurious bedrooms, and a conference and banqueting suite. At the same time the old coach-house was redeveloped into the Tavern Bar with informal dining and a terrace with a stunning view of the Lake. Work progressed efficiently, and the new facilities were opened in 1995 to great acclaim.

While the sporting side of the business flourished under Brian Bisiker, with continued investment in shooting and fishing (including the purchase of ten Bristol cutter boats) and new activities being introduced such as quad biking in 1996, the Hotel itself began to experience some difficulties. This led to the decision in 1999 to ring the changes by appointing Brian as Managing Director. The new millennium saw a new board and hotel team, which later in 2000 was headed up by experienced hotelier Anthony Rosser who continues in this position today. Widespread structural changes were made, systems computerised and contemporary practices introduced, which quickly resulted in a big improvement in the Hotel's fortunes.

A hallmark of Lake Vyrnwy Hotel has always been the care that it takes with the staff who ultimately determine the success of the business. Respect, training and a happy working environment sum up the Hotel's attitude to staff management. This led at this time to the building of twelve units of staff accommodation, which housed twenty-four members of staff.

Over the years since then the challenge has been to re-build the Hotel's infrastructure to make sure it remains fit for purpose for the future. The Victorian water supply, which came from a small reservoir on the hill above the Hotel in a one-inch pipe, was changed. With Brian driving the diggers, several hundred yards of new pipe were laid in order to connect the Hotel to the mains supply and storage tanks were installed with a capacity of 42,000 cubic litres. Over time and out of trading profits the electricity supply has also been enhanced and a new sewage system sufficient for a sizeable village was installed down the back drive.

As ever, challenges still presented themselves, not least the foot-and-mouth crisis of 2001 in which the initial outbreak nationally was confirmed at a farm only nine miles as the crow flies from Vyrnwy. The government of the time effectively closed the countryside and the Hotel was left with no business.

This contributed to the delay in development plans, but in 2004 the necessity for growth was identified by the management, which, due to the substantial investment in infrastructure, the Hotel was now in a strong position to deliver. A significant European grant was negotiated via the Welsh Tourist Board (now subsumed into the Welsh Assembly government) and an extension costing £2.75 million was built. It was opened in 2007 and consisted of fourteen new luxury bedrooms, a large function room and the Lake Vyrnwy Spa.

Due to this large investment in both facilities and people, the Hotel has prospered over the last decade and it now comprises fifty-two bedrooms, employs up to ninety members of staff (of whom forty live in Hotel-owned accommodation) and welcomes over twenty-six thousand sleeping guests a year. It is a major component of not only the economy of the Vyrnwy valley and community but of Mid-Wales overall. It also continues to thrive as a sporting hotel, constantly introducing new activities such as electric mountain bikes, but also ensuring the continuing success of its fishing and shooting. Not a bad 130-year journey for a small hunting lodge in Wales.

PART 3

The Sporting Side

CHAPTER SIX

Fishing the Lake: Historical Highlights

TROUT fishing started just two years after the Lake was finally completed and the waters were at full level in 1889. The first fishing trial before the formal opening of the fishery took place on 3 February 1891. The result was most encouraging. On the starting day, three trout were taken of good size: 1 lb 5 oz, 1 lb 3 oz and 1 lb 1 oz.

During the trial period covering February and the early part of March 1891, many trout of over the pound mark were caught. Messrs W. H. Avery, H. B. Harvey, A. P. Thornley and G. Ward were the pioneers. They took thirty-two fish weighing in total 29 lb 3 oz. The weather was appalling. The various gentlemen suffered an almost endless 'blizzard' and complained about how difficult it was to row boats in the prevailing conditions.

Fishing started in earnest on Good Friday 27 March 1891 in 'continuation of blizzard'. The beginning day attracted nineteen rods and in all 114 fish were caught, weighing an average of three quarters of a pound. Favourite flies during the first few months appear in the records as March Brown, Mallard & Claret and 'Black'. A trout of 2 lb was landed by 'The Turners'.

During 1891, a grand total of 4143 trout were caught with an average of just under the pound. Mr G. Ward, the first lessee of the Hotel, proved top of the fishermen's league with some 258 trout working out at 222 lb 12 oz. The Fishing Register was signed by 'Mr Durant Gibbings, Manager'.

After this auspicious start, trouting was in full swing on the Lake in the 1890s. Captain G. H. France took the best fish of 1892 of 2 lb 6 oz and over 18 inches long. Detailed records were kept again in 1893 with many trout of over a pound being taken. The largest fish caught that year was 2 lb 12 oz and the average weight of the 4340 fish ending on the Hotel tray was over 14 oz. In fact, the daily catch was displayed on trays between the bar and dining room, and later in the rod room, of the Hotel with slips showing the captors' names until only a decade or so ago, when food hygiene regulations sadly put an end to the practice.

It was also in 1893 that a great Victorian enthusiast Mr C. W. Gedney stayed at the Lake Vyrnwy Hotel and returned home to Bromley, Kent, to write a book entitled *Angling Holidays in pursuit of Salmon, Trout and Pike*. His work makes excellent reading today. The following extract from his book just has to be included in the Lake's angling history:

'The Lake teems with pound trout, and, although they are not so thick as to be "squeezing each other on the bank" like Pat's salmon, yet they are plentiful enough to yield a good basket every day to anyone who can fish at all with a two pounder, maybe at the head of the score. Yes, it is real good fishing, and I know of no other place where you can get anything like it.

There are two kinds of trout in the Lake – the aboriginal brownies, and the four thousand Loch Levens put in some years ago, which have thriven amazingly. What grand fighting fish Loch Levens are! My little ten-foot split cane rod – on which I have killed many 3 lb chalk stream trout in May Fly season – was no better than a child's toy against a pound Loch Leven in Lake Vyrnwy. I had to mount a substantial twelve-footer, and even then some of the fish took as long to kill as a fresh run sea-trout.

The Hotel is, in truth, replete with all the comforts of a well-ordered house, and a man who comes here on fishing bent, can be taken in and done for at an inclusive charge of three and a half guineas per week. Of this comfortable hostelry some grateful anglers have written, with poetic fervour:

We were out for a spin and we stopped at this Inn,
Where there's plenty of grub for inflating the skin,
The fishing was splendid; Miss Davies was good,
Stop if you can; we would if we could.

The lady immortalised in the foregoing verse is the manageress and the lessee of the establishment, and a real good one she is, too, as every grateful brother of the rod will testify who visits Lake Vyrnwy Hotel.'

One notable entry in the Register for 1894 appears in the entry for 3 September: 'Boatmen. 15 fish of total 12 lb for Duke of York's Luncheon'.

The chub 'menace', still present today, was first tackled in 1898. Food for the trout was becoming sparser as the acid water decimated plant life around the edge of the Lake and the management decided that the brownies could do without competition for it from the successful and exploding chub population. The Register mentions that on Tuesday 14 June 'Chubbing started today. Killed 1300 fish weighing one ton.' Despite such drastic action, chub still begin their spawning run in June and can often be seen in a large shoal at the head of Rhiwargor.

There was no 'limit' to the number of fish one could take in those early years. In 1899, the Reverend Gregorie and boatman caught forty-three fish in one day and Mr Garside topped this slaughter the next year with a colossal basket of forty-five fish reaching 38 lb – 'the best yet made on the Lake'. The cost of a day's fishing in 1922 was four shillings and you could have the 'sole use of boat, with man, per week for sixty shillings' while pheasant and duck shooting was one pound per day per gun in October and November.

During the first decade, the average weight of fish caught was around the 11 oz mark. A sharp drop to around half a pound or 8 oz started in 1906 and lasted at this level until a major effort was made to improve the fishery, starting in 1929. Stocking of the Lake was re-introduced that year and a nine inch limit finally brought in (today the limit is ten inches). Four thousand brown trout were put in plus one thousand rainbows.

The following March, Squadron-Leader Graham Martin, whose wife Belinda was the Hotel's proprietor, took further positive and, as it turned out, highly rewarding steps to upgrade the fishing. He took the best available advice and opted to try to supplement the trout's meagre food supply with snails and freshwater shrimps.

On 25 March 1930, 100,000 *Lymnea peregra* and 20,000 *Gammarus* (snails and shrimps) were laid down in suitable tributaries and bays and just a fortnight later another 50,000 snails were placed into the river at the top of Rhiwargor and other streams. Many tons of basic slag – to act as silt and fertiliser to encourage plant growth – were then dumped at the head of the Lake.

The outcome of all this expense and hard work proved highly gratifying. By 1934, the average weight was back to 10 oz and reached a satisfactory 13 oz by the outbreak of the Second World War. In 1936 nine rainbows of over 3 lb were taken during the season, quite a change in just six years.

The war meant a cessation of stocking for the duration, transport being the obvious problem. 'Soldiers may have taken considerable number of fish' is one terse comment in the Register. A further menace were the scores of cormorants that infested booms laid across the Lake to deter flying-boats or torpedoes fired at the dam in the wake of what the RAF had done to the

Ruhr and Möhne dams in Germany in 1943. Catching a really large fish became a rare event indeed, almost a once in a decade occasion.

That excellent, but now defunct, publication *The Fishing Gazette* carried many mentions of the Lake Vyrnwy fishery over the years. There is even a small lake in the woods behind the Boat House Pool at the back of Tower Hill named after the magazine. An experiment by the *Gazette* to raise large fish there and re-stock them into the main Lake was not a success.

Before then, an article had appeared in the 22 March 1913 edition of the *Gazette* by Walter Gallichan covering a particular Vyrnwy phenomenon, the Coch y bondhu or bracken beetle (*Phylopertha horticola*).

Gallichan also published a charming booklet about the fishing on the Lake, entitled *Lake Vyrnwy and Around: An account of a Welsh Highland, its sports, scenery and associations*, in 1912.

Apart from showing the tariff at the Hotel – at the time you could having fishing with boat and one man, including man's lunch and ale, for seven shillings per day – and some delightful pictures of the interior of the Hotel and Lake, he described Vyrnwy as 'the Loch Leven of Wales'. He also gives the reader a tour around the Lake. It is fascinating that today's fish favour exactly the same places as their forebears over a hundred years ago. His book is valid in every respect as a guide to fishing the Lake today – with the notable exception of the bracken beetle. Gallichan wrote:

'During the Fern-Web or Coch y bondhu season, from the end of June to about the third week of July, great execution may be done with the counterfeit fly. Mr Kennedy's floating beetle can be recommended in the Coch y bondhu season. It is a cunning imitation, and I speak from experience when I say that it is quickly seized by the trout in mistake for the real insect.'

Writing about the 1930s, Sir Edward Durand is concerned about the future of the beetle in his book *Wanderings with a Fly-Rod.* This is a real treasure and contains the most sound advice on fishing, proper behaviour – including handling fish – and where to find trout. He wrote:

'I think the days I really enjoyed most were late June and early July, when for a short time the Coch y bondhu beetle was coming off the hillside on to the water, but the fall of this tit-bit for the trout is a very chancy and uncertain event. The cork imitations, fished dry, of course, is a most amusing sport, and because of the weight, especially on fine gut, it is quite easy to break on the strike. Before the days of the increase of rainbows, which necessitated the use of stronger casts, it used to be a common event to leave the beetle in the fish's mouth, and as often as not he promptly spat it out again and then commenced the boatman's great game of 'Hunt the Beetle'.

I heard one amusing story first hand, from an exceedingly large and fine specimen of a fisherman, a veritable son of the Anak, who lost his beetle on the strike and, having spotted it later, discarded by the trout and floating on the surface, was rowed down to recover it. Just as his large hand was extended to pick it off the water a hungry trout rose and took it from between his fingers, and his surprise jump was nearly enough to upset the whole boat load, much to the alarm of the other occupants. Of course to be a real fishing story he should have caught the fish in his hand!

Unfortunately, the intensive planting of coniferous tress all around the Lake is, I fear, restricting and destroying the breeding-ground of the Coch y bondhu. Not only that but it is also seriously interfering with the sport of the inhabitants of the Hotel who come in the Autumn and Winter months for the shooting, because the enormous forests are growing up without rides or openings in them, making it impossible to beat them for game, besides harbouring all kinds of vermin which the keepers cannot get at to destroy.

The beetle is almost the May Fly of the Lake, and its possible extinction would be a very serious loss. The Coch y bondhu dry fly is very often successful before and after a fall of the real beetle, and is generally the most useful dry fly all season through.'

Edward Durand's concern for the Coch y bondhu has been fully justified. It is effectively gone and the last fisher, to my knowledge, to use the cork imitation with any great success (apart from around the Tower a few years ago at feeding time) was Michael Horton Ledger in the 1970s. Until the forests are cleared and the open moor allowed back in their place, we will not see it reappear.

It was Durand's book that started Sir John Baynes and his father Sir Roy on their love affair with Lake Vyrnwy back in 1946.

The Coch y bondhu was a highly popular bait – either as a fly or cork replica – for many years, although rather out of fashion today. Indeed, intrigued to see if it still worked, I called in at Hardy's, Pall Mall, in the early 1970s and asked an elderly assistant if the shop had any in stock. He thought for a moment and said:

'I doubt if we have any left. The last time I sold any of those was before the last war to a gentleman that used to fish a place called Lake Vyrnwy in Wales.'

Writing an article entitled 'Lake Vyrnwy: an introduction to newcomers' in the slim-line wartime *Fishing Gazette* in 1944, Colonel Dick Page also had some good things to say about the beetle. But he also drew our attention back to the chub, which he did not like at all. He wrote:

'A dry fly accepted by a chub is best sent to a dry cleaner if it is ever to float again. Chub are slimy to handle, difficult to kill and eject filthy green messes from both ends all over the boat in their death throes, and they eat much that would otherwise go to the trout.'

I also wrote about the Vyrnwy chub in the *Trout and Salmon* magazine thirty years ago. My view was not quite so jaundiced since a 3 lb chub in deep water can put up a tough, if somewhat stolid, fight. I know this since I caught three chub one afternoon and spent quite a while trying to kill them. Proudly, I carried them back to the Hotel and displayed my specimens on the fish tray outside the bar for a joke. An elderly female guest stopped by the tray on her way into dinner that evening and exclaimed at the great size of the chub compared with some brownies alongside. She prodded one of the chub. It was a mistake. All three suddenly came to life and leapt off the tray with a good deal of flapping and noise. The old lady nearly passed out with shock and had to retire upstairs for the rest of the evening. I was not popular.

After the Second World War, when the lease on the Hotel and sporting rights were taken on by ex-RAF Wing Commander James Moir and his wife, Ruth, getting the fishing and shooting back on track after the predations of war became a labour of love for him. He managed to put Vyrnwy firmly back on the sporting map.

The Westropp family guide to the Lake during those early visits to Vyrnwy in 1946–48 was Richard Threlfall's slim volume, entitled *Notes on Trout Fishing in Lake Vyrnwy and the Upper*

Vyrnwy River. It was something of a bible to my parents, Edward and Mary Westropp, and we were in awe of the great man. Although I was very young, I remember him snatching the ex-tank aerial rod about to be used by my mother and hurling it to the ground by the Hotel porch announcing grandly 'No man can fish with that'. He was right. For at that moment a car swung round the top bend of the drive and flattened the grey metal rod into spaghetti.

Colonel Dick Page caught a trout just under 4 lbs near the Tower in 1952. It was the biggest fish taken on Lake Vyrnwy for over thirty years. His achievement, however, was quickly topped: the following year Mr F. Ledsam landed a fish of 4 lb 10 oz. The largest caught since the fishery started, his record breaker was 23 inches long and 13 inches in girth.

The famous drought of 1959 caused alarmists among the experts to state that the Lake would take at least two years to reach its full level once more. They were very wrong. Water was going over the dam again on Boxing Day 1959.

An unofficial report exists of a fish weighing a gigantic 7 lb 2 oz by Mr Norman Davies of Bala. He says he boated his huge fish just below Cedig but there is nothing in the Register to verify the catch even though the local paper recorded the achievement. It would seem likely – pure conjecture though – that this fish's normal habitat was around the Tower during the time fish were fed there and it had swum up to Cedig in search of more food. It was not until 1961 that the average weight of Vyrnwy trout rose above 8 oz again.

Ruth Moir's decision to go into partnership with Vyrnwy regular, keen shot and fisherman John Baynes in 1972 was good fortune for the fishing guests. John knew as much about the fishing on the Lake as anybody. He opened up Cedig and, occasionally, Llwyn Rhiw, as boat stations. He commissioned a report from the Salmon & Trout Association's biologist to help him with future stocking policy and introduced electric outboards too (see below). This opened up the whole Lake to the day fisher keen to explore new or underutilised drifts.

In 1978, the average weight reached the one-pound mark for the first time since the fishery pre-opening trial back in 1891. Credit for this was mainly down to the excellent stocking policy at that time. For example, thirty-six trout of over 2½ lb were caught in 1979 plus a brown of 5½ lb. Year followed year with the average weight approaching the magic one-pound mark. Feeding trout from the Tower played an important role here.

The nationwide drought of 1976 hit Lake Vyrnwy even harder than the long dry spell of 1959. The fishing certainly suffered. But, with the water level down more than thirty-two feet, a number of features of the old drowned Llanwddyn – situated off Cedig – were exposed for the first time since pre-flooding in 1889.

When Jim Bisiker purchased the Hotel and the sporting rights in February 1987, his son Brian Bisiker was given charge of the sporting side. He was keen to see the fishing improve further and he continued the policy of stocking the Lake with good-sized fish.

The ruins came into view again in the great drought of 1987. I stayed a week at the Hotel with my then small sons Edward and Kit in August and we spent hours exploring the empty lake bed in Eunant, off Cedig, and virtually the whole of Rhiwargor.

It was fitting that the centenary of the Lake in 1991 was a spectacular fishing year. The total catch was the highest since the early 1890s at just short of three thousand fish, and a monster rainbow of 7 lb 2 oz was taken.

Good levels of stocking continued during the early 1990s with the average weight of fish caught staying around the one-pound mark. However, there was a definite decline in numbers caught as rod effort dwindled from 1996 onwards. This, in part, was due to a lack of publicity in the angling press about the Lake Vyrnwy fishery and by 2000 only 596 trout were caught in the whole year.

John Roberts took over the sporting side when Brian Bisiker was appointed Managing Director of the Lake Vyrnwy Hotel enterprise and he experimented for a while with only stocking brown trout. Good-sized brownies were put in each year and that shows up well in the average weight of the fish taken from 2003 onwards. In both 2003 and 2007, the average weight climbed to a record 1 lb 2-plus oz for the first time since fishing started in 1891.

Recently, the catch return sheets that all fishermen must fill in at the end of each day have included a column each for the trout caught as well as those killed and taken. I regard this as a great step in conservation as, previously, many smaller fish were unnecessarily knocked on the head to boost the catch return. Being able to put back some fish and just keep those the angler really wants to take home is to be applauded. Of course, as only larger fish are taken and put on the scales, the average weight was bound to increase too.

Catch statistics show that Vyrnwy is still popular with anglers and there are plenty of fish to catch. The returns for 2016 report 1300 trout caught, of which only sixty-four were rainbows. Over 1600 were caught in 2017 and two hundred of these were rainbows. I guess there were some chub as well but there is no space on the catch return to report these.

Many fishers like rainbow trout. In Vyrnwy, rainbows will move while the native browns stay dour and down early in the season and in mid-summer. So, in 2008, rainbows were once again stocked into the Lake, including a few very large fish. More records for the fishery began to appear with fish over 8 lb taken and many of 6-plus lb.

Stocking of rainbows has continued every year since, but the number of brownies being put into the Lake has dropped to a minimum in recent years. With costs running now to several pounds per pound for brown trout, it has become uneconomical to try to stock such a large lake with them. The average size of all fish caught has fallen as a result and the reason why the native browns are mostly now smaller than the old Registers proclaimed becomes clear in the section below.

The ecology of Lake Vyrnwy

When John Baynes took over the fishery at the beginning of 1973, he wanted to understand much more about the fish, their struggle to survive and how he might make a difference. He invited Dr Margaret E. Brown, who was then biologist to the Salmon & Trout Association, to visit Vyrnwy and write a report, which he hoped would help him understand the most effective and rewarding future stocking policy for the Lake.

In the event, Dr Brown's report covered a wide spectrum of ecological and biological data. It made fascinating reading and reveals much about the Lake and its inhabitants. A good deal of what she discovered was previously unknown or at best only guessed at from experience. However, what she discovered supports what we anglers have all experienced over the decades. The following are some key extracts from the Dr Brown's report:

Comments on the Fauna Collected

'On 26 March, I visited sites around the Lake and three inflowing streams. At each sampling station, I examined stones and took a "kick sample" with a pond-net; I examined the animals collected in a white pie-dish and noted what species I found and how abundant they were.

Samples from the lake shore where the substratum was stones and boulders or sand yielded few or no animals. This type of shore presents a harsh environment, particularly where there are changes in the lake level. Much of the lake edge is of this type and will give very little in the way of food for trout.

Where the lake shore was of a more gentle slope, with muddy sand and stones and some plants growing in it, there were more animals than on stony shores.

Zooplankton was abundant in Rhiwargor and I caught two small chub at Heartbreak Bay; these were fat and had evidently found enough to eat. This type of lake shore will produce food for fishes though the fauna was not very rich. The fact that Rhiwargor Bay is considered a good fishing locality probably is related to the shallow water and greater productivity there.

On the inflowing streams, Eunant proved very disappointing even up the valley where I had expected to find plenty of stonefly and mayfly nymphs. Cedig had a poor fauna where it was shaded by trees but the small stream sampled just above the woodland had an excellent fauna. The Rhiwargor stream and its tributary had fair faunas but the animals were much less abundant than in the small Cedig tributary. The Rhiwargor and upper Cedig should provide food and suitable spawning for trout (and chub in Rhiwargor); the Eunant seems almost useless as a nursery. The tiny stream flowing into Heartbreak Bay had a poor fauna but better than the Eunant.

There is likely to be an indigenous population, spawning in the inflowing streams and moving into the Lake after one or more years. Many of the streams are shaded and have poor fauna. Eunant stream has a poor fauna in spite of not being shaded; this is probably because it is acid, at least at some times of year (since it is now recognised that streams with occasional pH values below 6 usually have a sparse fauna compared with similar streams with pH always above 6). It seems likely that the indigenous trout population is not very large – that is, it does not seem likely that the trout grow slowly because of overstocking.

I have annual lengths calculated from scales read by Dr Worthington in 1939:

Age in years	1	2	3	4	5	6
Length (inches)	1.8	3.9	6.8	9.0	10.3	11.6

based on 10 fish

This indicates a growth rate slower than in Bala (Llyn Tegid) where the fish reach 8½ inches at three years old and 10½ at four.

Trout growth rates are very much dependent on food supply. My investigations showed that the food supply in the Lake is very limited since much of the shore is unproductive and changes in water level must limit the productivity of the gently sloping, sandy-mud shores. There may at times be plenty of zooplankton but Vyrnwy with its soft water is likely to be unproductive of plankton and zooplankton is good food for smaller trout than larger trout.

The main source of food for large trout must be of terrestrial origin – blown off the surrounding land; this food also will encourage the fish to rise to flies cast by anglers.

Rough pasture with heather and bracken is quite a good source of terrestrial insects for trout. Plantations of conifers are a very poor source because foresters naturally try to keep the numbers of insects as low as possible. Beech and rhododendron are other species which produce few insects and so are not useful as sources of food for trout. The present use of the Vyrnwy catchment, mainly for forestry and largely for conifers, must have reduced the amount of terrestrial food available compared with the rough pastures that surrounded the Lake until the 1930s.

There is evidence from some continental streams that plantations of red cedar and Sitka and Norway spruce produce substances that are toxic to insects, possibly also to trout so that trout are scarce and grow slowly in streams flowing through these plantations and for several miles below them. It may be that plantations of spruce round Vyrnwy are discouraging the trout – but the volume of water in the Lake is so large that I do not think this can be an important effect. Streams flowing through these plantations would be of no use as nurseries for trout.'

It is very encouraging that the Vyrnwy forestry contractors are now planting new fir trees well away from the feeder streams for reasons referred to above and this will prove of considerable benefit to the fauna and flora of Vyrnwy in the years to come.

CHAPTER SEVEN

Fishing the Lake Today

LAKE Vyrnwy can be a tough place to fish. It can also be amazingly easy. So much depends on the weather, conditions and experience. But this magnificent Lake presents the type of angling challenge that brings the true lover of wild brown trout fishing back time and again.

There can be days when every brownie in Vyrnwy (and there must be tens of thousands of them) is on the move and others when there might not be a fish in the Lake. 'If you can catch a trout on Lake Vyrnwy, you can catch a trout anywhere,' local boatman Sim Carpenter said over sixty years ago, when he was patiently trying to teach me to cast. I have fished on many waters at home and abroad since then and still think he was right.

Lake Vyrnwy was, for years, the largest man-made reservoir in the British Isles. Its splendid masonry dam – Europe's biggest – Rhine-like straining tower and heavily wooded surrounding hills and crags, provide the angler with the perfect setting for his or her sport. In 1889, 1121 acres of the Llanwddyn Valley were finally flooded with thirteen million gallons of water. During the first years following the flooding, the Lake produced good trout of just over a pound on average. At odd intervals over the past hundred years or so – and particularly since 1980 – it has managed to repeat the performance.

Food is a vital factor in any trout fishery and that is just one of the problems for the Vyrnwy fish in their endless fight for survival. Initially, food was plentiful, as much of the valley now covered up by the present normal level of the Lake was farmland. After the first glut in the early 1890s, the trout had a much tougher time filling their stomachs and their average size dropped, as the original surface soil was washed away to leave bare rock. The dark acid peat water from the mountains destroyed all vegetation and, with a few exceptions, stopped essential growth of water weed. For the most part, throughout the four-and-a-half-mile length of Lake Vyrnwy, the shoreline is now plain Cambrian rock or shale beach with the sides shelving steeply away into deep water.

Vyrnwy is a long narrow lake with many bays and indentations served by torrent rivers and streamlets. There are, however, several larger bays, the most notable being Rhiwargor and Eunant, the major arms that branch at the top north-west end; Llwyn Rhiw / Hafod on the south bank and Cedig on the north shore.

Of these, Rhiwargor is the shallowest and is often half empty during the dry months of mid-summer. Since grass and weed tend to grow there virtually every season creating a reliable food supply, the trout are more numerous and are usually in better condition. The original River Vyrnwy also enters the Lake at the top of Rhiwargor, carrying with it more food for the fish. Other popular fishing spots are the sizeable streams that drop into the Lake at Cedig, Llwyn Rhiw and Eunant.

At the dam end, the two large tunnels diverting waters from the adjoining valleys of Afon Cownwy and Afon Marchnant and the stream into and out of the Boat House Pool can also be hot spots for trout. The fish incline to cluster around these and they are favourite spawning runs in October and November, when there is enough water in the Lake to allow the trout to go up.

What of the fishing? It varies considerably depending on location and the time of year.

Being eight hundred feet up in the Welsh hills, Vyrnwy can be a cold place in winter with the warmer weather of spring arriving several weeks later than in the lower-lying parts of the country. The water temperature is slow to rise with the trout just as slow to start moving. An early Easter can be a freezing experience.

Late April, May and June see a great improvement in both trout activity and sport. A very hot spell in mid-summer, however, can have a terrible effect on the fishing and an accompanying east wind puts every trout down. Vyrnwy fish really don't like high pressure and a good old-fashioned wet south-westerly wind is ideal at any time of the season, which runs from April until the end of September.

Izaak Walton's old angling rhyme works really well at Vyrnwy:

> *When the wind is in the North,*
> *The skilful fisher goes not forth,*
> *When the wind is in the East*
> *'Tis good for neither man nor beast,*
> *When the wind is in the South*
> *It blows the flies in the fish's mouth,*
> *When the wind is in the West,*
> *Then it is the very best.*

Late July and August can be tough months for the fisher as the brown trout turn very dour. September can be a cracking month on the Lake. The cooler weather and water temperature sharpen the trout's appetites once more and it is a wonderful place to enjoy the early autumn colours and light.

Obviously, the fishing is better where there is a fuller larder for the trout or in the rare bays where the water is shallower. So the places already mentioned are favourites of the regular Vyrnwy fisher: Rhiwargor, Cedig, Llwyn Rhiw and Eunant, by late April, when the sun falls on more of the bay. Lechwedd, the beach affectionately known as Mrs Morris's, and the Tower Beat are often excellent spots. Even the Boat House Pool has its fans, particularly when the Lake is too rough for either comfort or safety.

Vyrnwy is in so many respects far closer in character to a natural mountain lake (the lochs of the Scottish Highlands, for example) than the other man-made reservoirs like Rutland, Grafham, Chew and Bewl Water. These look and fish as differently from Vyrnwy as chalk and cheese.

A very high proportion of Vyrnwy brown trout are home-grown 'natives', having started their lives in the gravel of many feeder streams. Stocking might seem unnecessary due to the huge number of fish in the Lake. This is not the case. The Lake has to be stocked to some extent to maintain a head of reasonably sized fish. Without stocking, the average size of Vyrnwy's wild trout is 6 to 8 inches. There are exceptions to this in every bay or drift and a one-pound Vyrnwy brownie gives a very good account of itself.

Stocking new fish into the Lake started in the early years but in earnest from 1929. It has been an annual event ever since, with the exception of the Second World War years. Recently an average of over one-thousand-plus brown trout and rainbows have been entered, spread between March and May. Stock fish came from the Chirk Fishery Company for many years and more recently rainbow trout have been sourced from the Cotswolds. At odd times, good-sized rainbows – up to 3 lb and in 2008 much bigger than that – have been put in with some spectacular results, and North American brook trout during the 1980s as well. Since the rainbow is at heart a migratory fish, they seldom stay in the Lake for more than a season or two, no doubt going over the dam during spates.

It is interesting to see how the colour of the Vyrnwy trout differs from place to place. Those brown trout from the top of Rhiwargor are often paler-backed than those living around the laurels of Eunant. Fish lying under the many trees lining the banks, the Chapel beat for example, are distinctly dark, as are those of the deeper dam end or around the Tower. On a flat calm day in late summer, it is possible to lean over the dam wall and see fish swimming below you. And on a still early morning in the spring, there can be the amazing and magical sight of hundreds and hundreds of trout rises ringing the entire surface of the Lake.

Newcomers and guests often ask about the depth of a particular bay or drift. To the fisherman, it is important to know that when the Lake is full early in the season Rhiwargor, most of Cedig, Llwyn Rhiw and the bridge end of Eunant are shallow and will possibly be high and dry with a fair covering of vegetation by the end of an average summer. This is not the case, of course, in wet summers, when water can cascade over the dam for weeks, even in July and August. The fish, on balance, prefer to live in weedier environments or tucked under cover of the tree canopy along the banks when the waters return.

On the other hand, the height from the old drowned river bed near the dam to overflow level is eighty-four feet, the deepest part of the Lake. The great drought of 1959 caused a good deal of concern. It gradually became clear that Liverpool was about to lose its water supply as the Lake dried up. BBC News sent a television camera crew to film the amazing shrinking Lake, which resulted in huge traffic jams as trippers flocked to survey the scene.

A steel buoy can be seen floating a hundred yards or so off the Boat House Pool below the Hotel. This marks the valve that can draw water from the very deepest part of the Lake in the event of severe drought, stranding the beautiful straining tower. In 1959, it took divers two nervous weeks to locate and clear silt from the outlet and the Liverpool Waterworks Company determined that it would never be lost again.

Old hands at Vyrnwy use low water conditions to study the topography of the lake bed. All kinds of tumbled-down dry-stone walls, bridges and buildings come to light and, when the Lake is full again, these are all good holding places for fish. It is worth studying the original course of the river in Rhiwargor in times of drought. The natural current, although hardly discernible, follows this path even today when Vyrnwy is at overflow height.

Bird lovers among the anglers are in for a double bonus when fishing at Rhiwargor, this most scenic arm of the Lake. In 1977, the Royal Society for the Protection of Birds (RSPB) established the Lake Vyrnwy Reserve there. This was created following a 1973 agreement by the Severn Trent Water Authority, the RSPB, the Forestry Commission and the Lake Vyrnwy Hotel, as the sporting tenants. The Reserve covers sixteen thousand acres, with the north-west of the Lake as a focus.

Dozens of varieties of water and upland birdlife can be seen in the Reserve or from a boat. The most obvious sign of the RSPB presence is the large bird hide tucked away on the island at the top of Rhiwargor and the hide on the north shoreline at Bailey's Point. Both are well signposted and are approached by attractive lakeside woodland paths.

How to fish Lake Vyrnwy

Lake Vyrnwy is a 'fly-only' water and has to be fished from a boat, usually drifting loch-style with a team of three flies. Vyrnwy trout tend to be found very close to the shore. So, the key to catching fish on the Lake is always to try to get your flies as near the stones as possible. Never miss an opportunity to cast under over-hanging trees if they are between you and the bank.

Beginners often drift either across the Lake or many yards out from the shore. I have been out with a fellow angler who, despite the strongest advice from me and the very experienced man at the oars, insisted we drift straight down the centre of the Lake between the Tower and the dam. He was adamant that this technique usually worked on Rutland Water and we might be missing a trick at Vyrnwy. We ended the day fishless. Another boat hugging the bank came home with a bag of five brace, all caught in two hours.

An increasing number of Midlands reservoir fishers do well on lures fished on sinking or sink-tip lines, especially early in the season. Stick with it if that works for you but otherwise try fishing smaller and shallower.

Flies

The really big question every fishing day is what fly to put on the end of the leader. Most people use three flies, with the top or 'bob' fly tending to be bushy or, at least, bushier than the other two, and the tail or end fly often slightly heavier with some flash in the tying. A list of flies that have attracted trout at Lake Vyrnwy over the years would be very long indeed. But fashions change with new designs, fly-tying materials and hooks so I have made a selection of wet and dry flies, nymphs, as well as lures, to suit every taste and fishing technique:

Wet Flies

Alexandra	Invicta
Bibio	Mallard & Claret
Black Pennell	Peter Ross
Butcher	Zulu
Connemara Black	

Dry Flies

Claret Bumble	Coch y Bondhu
Greenwell's Glory	G&H Sedge
Grey Wulff	

Nymphs

Buzzers Black/Red	Damsel Nymph
Diawl Bach	Pheasant Tail

Lures

Black Chenille	Montana
Sweeney Todd	Viva

A good rule for choosing a fly at Vyrnwy is: when in doubt, go for black. My leader in the early months will be a team of three small black or darkish wet flies, size 12. Black lures, like the Montana or Viva, work well early on as well. I will be a little more adventurous by late May and include an Invicta or maybe a Peter Ross for a sunny day. The Diawl Bach has firmly established itself as a favourite over the past fifteen years or so and scores well for trout under the trees along the shore.

There is always one pattern each month that is 'in vogue'. A successful fisherman reports back that he has taken all his fish on a 'Green Wonder', or whatever, and everybody else immediately adds the fly to their team. The odds in favour of that particular fly working therefore automatically rise. It will stay the favourite until somebody else makes a killing on a 'Black Wonder' and the whole pattern happens all over again.

So, fish the 'in' fly but never abandon the traditional successful patterns solely for the new 'killer' pattern.

Getting started for the day

Virtually all trout fishing on Lake Vyrnwy is from a boat. At high water, there are no beaches or shoreline from where you can cast a line and just a couple when the water is lower: Mrs Morris's Beach at Lechwedd and just north of the Boat House Pool at the end of the Tower drift.

Always call ahead to the Hotel when planning a fishing trip to Vyrnwy (telephone 01691 870692) to book your boat for the session (they cannot be booked online). All fishers need report to the Hotel reception at the start of their day to pick up their fishing permit and find out the number and location of their boat. Most people hire an electric outboard motor and accompanying large battery to power them around the Lake, although a few still prefer to row themselves from drift to drift. Engines and batteries – and mandatory lifejacket – are available and put out just by the main hotel porch. Remember to ask for the combination lock number to free the oars before setting off down to the lake.

There are two boat stations. The Boat House Pool is easiest to find. It is situated at the bend at the bottom of the Hotel drive and parking is just above the boat pontoon. The other, Whitegates, is located in the Rhiwargor arm some four miles on from the Boat House Pool and half a mile from the top.

Which boat station is better? The records show that there is no difference in fish catches per rod day. The Boat House Pool at the dam end of the Lake is probably where the beginner should start at Vyrnwy. There are lots of landmarks – the dam, the Tower and the two tunnels – and good long drifts. The wind is also less fickle and there is always the Boat House Pool itself to run to for sanctuary if conditions turn rough.

Whitegates and the Rhiwargor and Eunant bays are very scenic and, I reckon, hold more free rising trout. However, getting down to the boats and carrying both gear and battery is definitely more testing. The winds can often be contrary due to the north-west lie of the Lake and the height of the hills at that end. It also rains more there by several inches a year than the dam end.

Weather conditions at Vyrnwy can change with alarming speed. They can be appalling or brilliant. The valley appears to have a weather pattern all of its own. It can be pouring with rain at Vyrnwy and bright sunshine just nine miles down the hills at Llanfyllin or vice versa. Basically, Vyrnwy is a very wet place. The engineers from Liverpool Corporation would not have chosen the valley to build their reservoir if it were not. The average rainfall over the last century is an impressive 75 inches. Rhiwargor gets, on average, 12 inches more rain per year than the dam end.

Winds are so variable that they can change direction several times a day. At the Eunant–Rhiwargor point by the 'Oaks', the wind can hit you from two directions at once creating rather confusing fishing conditions. Water spouts are not unknown when a good westerly is blowing. And, inexplicably and infuriatingly, the wind will die altogether and a mirror-like quality overtakes the Lake. The unpredictability of the wind at Vyrnwy is due to a combination of its geographical lie – south-east to north-west – and its topography, with many gaps in the surrounding hills. So, while the blow may be up the Lake from the dam end in a prevailing south-westerly, it may be coming in exactly the opposite direction out of Eunant or Rhiwargor.

An unnecessarily gloomy picture may have been painted here. On the other side of the coin, I assure you that Vyrnwy pulls some really spectacular warm cloudless dry weeks out of the bag. Come prepared for anything from a heatwave to a blizzard. Warm and waterproof coat, hat and over-trousers are all mandatory equipment; Wellington boots are a good idea too. Leave your waders at home – you will not need them.

The boats

A word or two about the boats. Please tie up your boat when you come off the water at the end of an outing. Always double check that the chain is utterly secure. So many boats have been smashed to bits on the rocks overnight simply because people forgot, or did not bother, to hook the chain firmly to the rings on the Boat House Pool pontoon or the cross-timber at Whitegates. Stow the oars so that the blades are inside the boat and the combination lock wire is secure.

There are a couple of golden rules for those who hire the Hotel's excellent and silent-running electric outboards. Always think of the storage capacity of the battery before motoring grandly three miles or so downwind. Vyrnwy batteries go flat like any others. Rowing a boat against a strong wind and rough wave for several miles is not recommended. Never switch on the engine with a line nearby in the water. Thousands of expensive lines have been wound around propellers to destruction. The Lake has a rocky shoreline so think of the propeller whenever starting from the mooring point or near the bank. The drive shaft

17. Ruth and Jamie Moir who took over the running of the Hotel in 1947.

18. John and Roy Baynes with their fishing catch, 1948.

19. A shooting party and beaters outside the Hotel in the 1950s.

20. John and Ida Thomas with Alice Carpenter and Miriam Probert standing outside the Tavern in the early 1970s.

21. The Baynes family at the Hotel in early 1980s: *from left*, Christopher, Simon, John, Shirley, Tim and William.

22. Brian Roberts, Brian Bisiker and John Roberts in the late 1980s.

23. A shooting lunch in the 1980s.

24. Brian and Mabel Roberts (*fifth and sixth to the right at the front*) on Brian's last day as Head Keeper in 1997.

25. George Westropp at Mrs Morris's Beach in May 2009.

26. Fishermen on the Lake today.

27. Linda Roberts' retirement in 2018 after 59 years working at the Hotel.

28. Photograph from an article in the *County Times* of the Jones family – Paul, Evelyn and Selwyn – celebrating 85 years of service to the Hotel in 2000. Paul still works for the Hotel today and the family's combined length of service now stands at 112 years.

29. The Hotel provides stunning views even in midwinter.

30. One of the Hotel's bedrooms with a spectacular view of the Lake.

31. & 32. Aerial views of the Hotel today taken by David Jones of Fotosfromsky.com.

flips up easily out of the water with minimum effort so use oars when first getting underway or just before docking.

A fishing tour of the Lake

The sheer size of the Lake can be daunting to the first-time fisher on Vyrnwy. Until Rutland Water was built in the 1970s, Vyrnwy was the largest lake in England and Wales with twelve miles of shoreline and dozens of bays and features. It is not an easy place to fish without a guide.

Boat House Pool to Whitegates

The Boat House Pool may be the first encounter with the Lake for most fishers, especially if the water level is high. We will start our fishing tour from there.

From the dock, row a couple of strokes up the Pool and let the boat drift quietly, casting under the bushes and trees at either side. When the Lake is full, the shallows at the top end of the Pool can be very good. Motoring or rowing out from the Pool under the bridge into the main body of the Lake, I am going to take you on an anti-clockwise tour of the shoreline.

A rock promontory juts out into the Lake just eighty yards from the bridge and you should be prepared for fish almost immediately. There is a gravelly beach around the point – where boats are often moored when the Pool is high and dry in the summer – and the water is all worth fishing from there to the Tower. Always cast as close as you can to the shoreline and this will prove doubly important when there are overhanging branches.

The Tower usually holds good numbers of fish on the down-wind side of the arches linking the structure to the road. A number of years ago, the Tower keeper used to feed the trout at 11am each morning and a large, hungry shoal gathered in anticipation of an early lunch. With automation of the Tower, the days of two men working the impressive Victorian straining machinery each day are gone and the feeding stopped.

If the wind is in the south or east, the next hundred yards after the Tower will be worth attention. I have seldom had much success over the next three-quarters of a mile and tend to row straight on to within five hundred yards of the next big bay: Cedig. The water shallows and many fish hold around Cedig Bay. Later in the spring, this will be a good place for rainbow trout. It is easy to find as you will drift past some carved wooden dolphins and a public picnic area.

Cedig itself can be outstanding. My sister, Maggie Vaux Sims, and I had seventeen fish in an hour there one morning in late March and the water always holds a good head of trout. Again, fish as close as you can to the shoreline and it is always worth pushing a line right into the bushes where the Cedig River enters the Lake.

Take the time to look up while in the bay at the giant Douglas fir trees, now named the 'Vyrnwy Giants'. Until 2006, one of the huge Cedig firs was officially the tallest tree in Britain but there is now another Douglas contending for that crown in Perthshire, Scotland.

Fishing on and out of Cedig, the shoreline is shallow and can be good at all times of the year. There are a couple of hundred yards of willow bushes growing in the water before the stone lined bank reappears under sycamore trees. Stocked rainbows and natural browns seem to like this shoreline, so fish it thoroughly until arriving half a mile later at Lechwedd or Mrs Morris's Beach. Pay close attention to this whole area and particularly off the beach. Incidentally, when you have fished the area it is a useful place for a picnic or a stop for a cup of tea. It is identified by the prominent beach in low water with a house on the hill above it.

Sycamores and willow continue to grow over the bank and in the shallows for the next four hundred yards and provide a wonderful drift, especially for the bank-side rod. The shore steepens after that and I usually do not do so well for a couple more hundred yards until arriving at the next important inlet called Fynnant. Two small streams enter the Lake there hidden by many large willow trees and bushes and I seldom drift it without at least one taker. Pay serious attention to Fynnant.

The willow bushes as you round the corner towards the Chapel and Chapel drift are worth covering, casting alongside and flicking under large sycamore trees. It holds many small fish and there is often movement under the trees. Try to fish as close into the rocks as you can.

The Chapel has been a favourite of mine for decades for the evening rise. It also provides a great place to get out of the wind and rain at lunchtime on rough days. The Chapel itself is one of the very few buildings from Old Llanwddyn to survive the inundation of 1888–89 and contains some very touching pencil graffiti from soldiers on leave from both the First and Second World Wars.

From there to the boat station at Whitegates should also be drifted but do not dally unless fish are on the move. In May and June, you will frequently see scores of fish rising well out from the bank and these are invariably the large shoals of chub, which spend the spring between the Chapel and Eunant before moving up the Lake to the top of Rhiwargor in the summer.

The chub can grow to 4 lb in Vyrnwy and will take a small fly. If you have not caught one before, they take lightly and then bore down in the water in a good and solid fight. The Whitegates Beach is definitely worth fishing over, although beach may be too generous a word, as most of it is covered by willow and alder bushes until the small area where the boats are moored.

Rhiwargor to Eunant

Just around the trees from Whitegates is a bay that every boat seems to cover when setting out for a day from the top end of the Lake. They are right to do so at any time of the season.

You are now in Rhiwargor, where the Lake will shrink in drier summer conditions. When the water is low, the top four hundred yards of the Lake will be almost unfishable but, when water allows, thoroughly cover the whole of the top end from Bailey's Point – named after Judge Desmond Bailey who fished Vyrnwy for more than sixty years – to the Island. It holds more fish than anywhere else on Vyrnwy. Being shallow, it is the one place on the whole Lake that you can drift right across the middle and never be more than four or five feet from the Lake bed. Fish will take anywhere.

Bailey's Point is easy to find as the RSPB bird hide is located on the edge of the water there. The larger bird hide can be found behind the Island at the end of the Lake just five hundred yards away, but is not visible when fishing. One of the best drifts is to line yourself up with the end of Bailey's Point and drift diagonally into the reeds by the river mouth at the very top of Rhiwargor if the wind is coming from the south or east – or vice versa for a north or north-west wind. A west wind causes great confusion to the boat handler here as the wind swirls in every direction and a drift becomes almost impossible.

Rhiwargor is the most scenic arm of the Lake and is a firm favourite with many regulars, including me. The cliffs of Eunant Moor to the south and the northern bluffs around Alt-Forgan are more reminiscent of the Canadian Rockies than mid-Wales.

The Upper Vyrnwy River enters Rhiwargor top left and holds many good trout. The abundant fry spawned and hatched in the river attract larger fish and these cannibals are easily identifiable by their larger heads and long streamlined shape. A drift into and around the willows growing at the mouth of the river can prove worthwhile with a favourable wind. You will probably find a shoal of chub there in the high summer months.

The south shore of Rhiwargor is tempting but fairly non-productive after the first excellent two hundred yards. I recommend rowing or drifting at a reasonable speed down the whole half mile length, until you get near the point joining Rhiwargor and Eunant. Oak trees hang over the rock point and there are always fish under the trees. The Oaks were a favourite of many of the Lake's top fishers over the years, including Michael Horton Ledger and Judge Bailey. These two teamed up for nearly twenty Easters and invariably came in with full baskets despite gales, snow or freezing rain. The secret of their daily limit catch of ten fish each: small dark flies.

Around the corner and past the Oaks into Eunant I find the right-hand north shore-line disappointing. However, you will notice an island covered in small bushes at the top end of the bay near the road bridge. This is the site of Eunant Hall, which was demolished just before the flooding a hundred or so years ago, and the trout appear to enjoy the shallow water and rocks among the ruins here.

To the south of Eunant Bridge, rhododendron bushes grow for two hundred yards and this is a popular haunt of rainbow trout in the late spring and early summer, and the odd chub too. Work along the bushes and back out to the Hall ruins. It is always worth shooting a line under the bridge itself as you drift past.

If the sun is shining, the drift from the bridge along the half-mile curved southern wooded shore of Eunant back to the main body of the Lake can be spectacular for native browns. In May, fish can move to virtually every cast and a dry fly flicked under the overhanging tree branches can work well. Because of the lie of this bay, the wind can blow in three or four directions in just a few minutes or just be flat calm. It is difficult to get a regular drift but the innovation of the electric motor or colleague to row quietly along the side prove invaluable.

Eunant to the Boat House Pool

Just before drifting around the corner out of Eunant into the main Lake again, there are a hundred yards or so of large laurel bushes and a few rhododendrons. Trout like the dark cover provided by the bushes. Spend time fishing this stretch carefully. The laurels should be worth it.

The shore then becomes very steep as you drift on down the Lake, with high rocks climbing straight up to the road above. Although the water is obviously deep, the drift from there down to where the point of Llwyn Rhiw juts out into the Lake is as good as any for brown trout. It looks uninviting and most fishers pass it by. This is a mistake.

When the brownies start to move in late April, May and early June, the Eunant – Llwyn Rhiw drift can be most exciting. I have had several baskets of fifteen fish or more in an afternoon working this stretch.

Llwyn Rhiw is shallow and you may discover fish across the whole of this pretty bay. On windy days, it can be a useful haven but it is not a place to run out of battery power if you have set out from any of the two normal boat stations. It is a two-mile row back to Whitegates or just short of three to the Boat House Pool. Crossing the Lake on a windy day can be quite alarming with waves several feet high.

I have never caught a fish in the mouth of the Hafod River at the top of Llwyn Rhiw so concentrate on the drift between the river and the large culvert three hundred yards down the Lake.

Given reasonable wind conditions, the long mile-and-a-half drift from there to Ceunant Bridge, with its waterfall, is good for smallish browns and well worth working down. To get your bearings, Ceunant Bridge is almost exactly opposite Cedig Bay at the widest part of the Lake.

Drifting on for the next half mile until Heartbreak Bay – so called because it looks so intriguing and fishy – is unremarkable, except for the public picnic area near Llechwedd-du farmhouse. I usually motor straight through this area to avoid day trippers and people throwing sticks for dogs. This is one rare spot on Lake Vyrnwy where the public can easily get down to the shoreline and they take full advantage of the opportunity. There are always fish along this stretch, but nothing spectacular. Heartbreak Bay itself seldom comes up to expectations. I avoid it.

We are now drifting on to approach some rocks – featuring a well-concealed Second World War defensive pillbox – before turning the corner to the old Corporation Boat House and Cownwy Tunnel. The rocks are worth covering but prepare to row through the next section as it features a launching ramp for canoes and sailing boats. It is a little disconcerting to find yourself surrounded by young people in bright orange canoes while drifting, as you think, quietly and peacefully along.

It is worth fishing around the Cownwy Tunnel – canoes, sailing boats and buoys permitting – and then quickly fish down to the dam. There is a good chance of picking-up or turning a fish as you do so.

My usual routine is to move straight onto the dam and, if lucky, discover the foam lines some ten or twelve feet from the dam wall. Rainbows seem to lurk below the foam line eating dead flies and other food blown down the Lake. Casting right up to the dam wall with a long line and fishing slowly and steadily back to the boat is often rewarding.

From the dam to the next tunnel – the Marchnant – can be a reasonable drift if the wind is not too strong from the south-west. It can also be a bit disconcerting since it is alongside the road where so many visitors to Vyrnwy first park to take their photos before driving around the Lake. You can be assured of an appreciative audience if you happen to catch a fish there.

The Marchnant Tunnel area is invariably worth a cast or two. At high water and exactly opposite the mouth of the tunnel, you can see a pinprick of white light from the far end, a mile and a half through the mountain under the Hotel. At the other end is the Marchnant Pool and each November hundreds of brown trout swim through on their spawning run. I have seen the ledges leading to the opening on the lakeside grey with fish waiting for the right time and conditions to run in the late autumn.

It is now just three hundred yards or so back to the Boat House Pool from here and the end of the round Lake Vyrnwy fishing tour. It can be a grand last drift with many newly stocked fish settling among the rocks and gravel just off the shore. Please note the large steel buoy floating a little way out from the bank and its attendant cormorants. They would not be there if there were no fish.

A final reminder. Do resist the temptation to fish in the middle of the Lake, with the exception of the shallows at the top of Rhiwargor or around the island at the head of Eunant. You will probably waste your time.

How long does it take to fish around the entire Lake? Back in the 1970s and 80s, one fisher would motor around the whole twelve miles of shoreline in a single day once a week with his electric outboard. I reckon it should take three days to drift every inch of the shoreline of Vyrnwy but it can be done in two, given reasonable winds.

How many fish can you take each day from Lake Vyrnwy? The catch limit for some years past has been four, and no fish under ten inches may be killed. After the limit, catch and release is permitted. In the case of undersized trout that must be put back, do so as gently as you are able.

CHAPTER EIGHT

Shooting at Lake Vyrnwy: 1890–1947

Beginnings: 1890–1919

HAVING purchased the extensive estate surrounding the new reservoir, the Liverpool Corporation had to consider how to take advantage of its sporting potential. As well as establishing the fishery, measures were put in hand to let the shooting rights to a suitable tenant. Given the relative inaccessibility of Lake Vyrnwy in those days, people coming to shoot were bound to require accommodation, and so it was natural to involve the Hotel in the shooting scene, as well as the fishing, from the start.

As explained earlier, the estate was gradually built up to cover twenty-three thousand acres. From the sporting angle it was divided into two parts: the grouse moors, forming a rough horse-shoe around the northern end of the Lake, and the low-ground shooting. On the south-west side, on the moor known as Mynydd St John, the Earl of Powis retained the shooting rights, as did Sir Watkin Williams-Wynn over the land he had sold on the eastern side.

While the lessees of the Hotel appear to have been given first refusal over renting the grouse moors, the lease of them was kept separate from that of the low-ground shooting, as could be seen in the wording of the advertisement quoted in Chapter 4. Although no lessee did ever refuse to take the moors, there was the opportunity to do so. Needless to say, they were a valuable asset to the business, as the Hotel needed every bit of 'drawing-power' to bring customers to its isolated situation.

An idea of what was available to a guest in 1912 can be seen

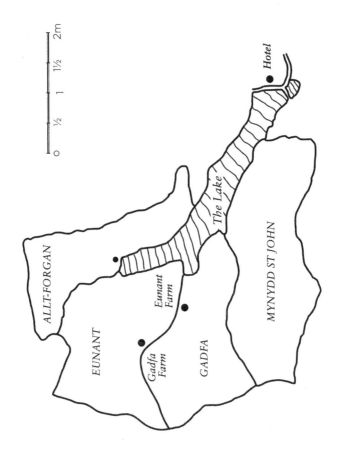

The Grouse Moors

ALLT-FORGAN

EUNANT

Gadfa
Farm

Eunant
Farm

GADFA

The Lake

MYNYDD ST JOHN

Hotel

0   ½   1   1½   2m

in this extract from W. M. Gallichan's book *Lake Vyrnwy and Around*:

'SHOOTING

The tract of country within the shooting rights of the Hotel covers about 40,000 acres. The greater part of the preserve consists of grouse moors, of which there are four, each one extensive and well stocked. Grouse thrive on the Berwyn Mountains, the high situation and the vegetation, especially the great acreage of heather, being extremely favourable for their increase. No better grouse moors can be found in Wales, nor even in the Kingdom, than those heath-covered uplands between Llangollen and Lake Vyrnwy. The country is well adapted for walking-up the birds with dogs or for driving the grouse.

Close to the Hotel is a big moor, reserved for shooting visitors. Grouse may be put up within a few hundred yards of the house, and there are plenty of rabbits and a few hares on this beat. The total bag of grouse for the season of 1908 was eight hundred brace.

The many coverts on both sides of the Lake harbour a large number of pheasants, and interesting shooting may be enjoyed in the coppices at the further end of the water, and in the numerous plantations and hanging woods on the estate. Rabbits breed in large numbers almost everywhere up to a height of about one thousand feet, and they are especially abundant around the Lake where the herbage is green and sweet.

Woodcock are frequently shot around Lake Vyrnwy. Snipe, both common and jack-snipe, visit all the morasses, marshes and pools of the district. Here and there the gunner will meet with coveys of partridges in the low-lying parts of the preserve. Blackcock are not common in any part of Wales, but there are a few in the neighbourhood of Llanwddyn.

The gunner will vary his bag with an occasional wood-pigeon or plover. Curlews breed on the Berwyns, and visit the range in considerable flocks. Golden plovers are visitors to the moors, and breed on the Berwyns.

Hard weather brings a varied company of wildfowl to the Lake and the district around. Geese are often seen on the water, and wild swans are visitors. Ducks of several species resort to the sheet of water, and flocks may be seen almost every day, while there are regular nesting places on the islets and around the shores. Sheldrakes sometimes appear on the Lake; teal, widgeon and mallards also visit the locality.'

The figure of forty thousand acres is accounted for by the fact that the Hotel rented extra moorland from Sir Watkin Williams-Wynn, and a lot of low-ground shooting on farms in the direction of Llanfyllin, in addition to the rights taken from the Lake Vyrnwy estate.

The four moors mentioned are the three main ones known as Gadfa, Eunant, and Allt-Forgan, plus the moor immediately north of the Hotel, which today is barely recognisable as such. Grass has now replaced most of the heather, and a large area is covered by forestry. Grouse have not been seen there for twenty years.

While the moor near the Hotel was, as Gallichan reports, 'reserved for shooting visitors', the three main ones were sub-let to either syndicates, or individuals, depending on circumstances.

Naturally those who took the grouse shooting were expected to stay in the Hotel. Mr G. G. Barker rented Allt-Forgan moor for some years at the turn of the century, and brought his party of friends and relations to stay at the Hotel. His son, Brigadier C. N. Barker was some years ago able to recognise some of the places shown in his father's old photo-albums while fishing at the northern end of the Lake below Allt-Forgan mountain.

Up to 1914 the total number of grouse shot each year averaged eight hundred brace or more. During the First World War, this average fell to less than half, the total for 1917 being 355 brace. The reasons were set out very clearly in a letter from William Hampson to Lieutenant-Colonel J. R. Davidson, DSO, the Liverpool Corporation water engineer, on 4 September 1918. This was one of several letters, already referred to in an earlier chapter, that were written at the time in connection with the search for someone to take over the Hotel when Hampson's lease expired in 1919. Mr Caley, negotiating on behalf of the syndicate that eventually did take over, had clearly been running down the moors in hopes of lowering the rent:

'As regards the moors, they [the syndicate] seem to think because the present tenant has made such small bags, the moors will never realise the pre-war rents. Mr Docker has taken the moors at much less than half the pre-war rent, £300 as against £680, and he knew quite well it has been impossible to do the usual keepering. Up to 1914 I had four keepers, three of them joined the Army as volunteers and one has been killed in action in France.

I can give you very good reasons why the present tenant's bags have been so small, and I am assured by my keeper there is a very good stock of birds in the moors at the present time. But if the war lasts much longer I am afraid serious damage will be done to the moors by vermin –

for so many keepers are killing vermin in another form in France.'

The one keeper left was Tom Hughes, who spent most of his working life on the Vyrnwy estate, from about 1892 up to 1937.

During the war, two measures were put in hand that were not helpful for the long-term grouse prospects on the moors: the numbers of sheep were increased as part of the war effort, and a programme of planting more trees around the edge of the moorland areas was started. A certain number of pheasants were reared on the low-ground each year up to the war, but never on the scale that was to become the practice in later years.

1919–1947

In 1919 William Hampson retired, and the syndicate comprising Messrs Caley and James and Major J. G. Lowndes took over the lease of the Hotel.

About two years after the changeover, Major Lowndes, the most active member of the syndicate, became incensed at the loss of lambs on the farm due to the depredations of foxes. He therefore started a small pack of hounds, which were kennelled in a wooden shed in the Hotel grounds. It was a foot pack, supported by men with guns, who were placed at strategic points around woods and coverts in order to shoot any foxes that were pushed out by the hounds. A worker on the estate wrote a poem about a hunting day, describing Major Lowndes, who always rode to the meets. Written first in Welsh, it was put into English by the school-master in Llanwddyn:

> *The day for hunting Reynard*
> *Wakes up the countryside,*
> *When the Major to the hunting field*
> *With Vyrnwy's pack doth ride.*

He's off to mount Ty-Uchaf
With shouts of "Tally-ho",
And he's humming at the canter
"A hunting we will go".

Hark! Listen to the horn
And answer to its call
For Mr Hill is shouting
"On guard!" you gunners all.

And now the hounds are prowling
In forest, field, and fen,
Intent to find old Reynard
And drive him from his den.

The Corporation workers
Think of the day with joy,
And wonder in the morning
Who'll be the lucky boy.
The lucky one at watch
Concealed behind a bush,
Who'll shoot the cunning creature
And carry home his brush.

Mr Hill, the farm bailiff, also rode to the meet, accompanied by his daughter Ruby, who held the three horses while hunting was in progress.

The shooting during the inter-war years was conducted on similar lines to that established before 1914, but the emphasis altered as the bags of grouse shot on the moors never recovered to the average figures expected earlier. The result was that the low-ground shooting was given more attention, and the numbers of pheasants reared was steadily increased. In addition to the reared pheasant shoot, often let to a syndicate, there was an extensive rough shoot, kept for small parties of guns or individuals staying in the Hotel.

In a book entitled *Shooting Ways and Shooting Days*, J. C. M. Nichols produced an account of how the rough shoot was operated in the 1920s:

'Quite the best shooting hotel I have stayed at is the well-known Lake Vyrnwy Hotel in North Wales, at which I made a short stay in October, 1929. They do you well; and anyone who is not afraid of hard work, i.e. walking hills which could well be called mountains, and content with a modest bag of say six to ten head of wild grouse or equally wild pheasants, might find much to please him at Vyrnwy.

The Hotel shootings ran to (I believe) some 20,000 acres of moors and woodlands for the accommodation of shooting guests. There was also an extensive acreage of "driving" moor which was usually let by the season.

Our usual procedure (two guns) was to go out with a keeper who, with his retriever and two spaniels, would work the higher moorland; sometimes posting the guns forward, or again himself taking the crest of the hills, with the guns walking a flank along some tiny goat-path or as best they could. Every now and again a grouse or outlying pheasant would be flushed, to come rocketing out across the valley, and giving perchance a wonderful high curling shot to one or other of the guns. The shooting was rendered doubly difficult as quite probably one would be caught negotiating an extra steep bit, with one foot a yard higher than the other.

Should I revisit Vyrnwy, I think my age and dignity would require the services of one of those sturdy little Welsh shooting-ponies, of which the Hotel stables held some half-dozen or more. There were a few partridges to be found on the lower ground, and on the hills we generally flushed two or three blackcock. We were told that these fine birds were much scarcer than they had been a few years previously.

Talking of Vyrnwy reminds me of one of the best retrieves I have ever seen. Towards the end of a long day's tramp, a pheasant had been just wing-tipped and dropped into some of the roughest undergrowth, a very lively runner. Jones, the keeper, was engaged in beating; and his dog, a black Labrador, could not be given the line till some minutes afterwards.

We sat down to smoke a pipe and give the dog time to work, and finally as dusk was falling, prepared to start on our homewards walk. I then caught sight of a black dot coming towards us from a tremendous distance over the hill. "Here's your dog at last," I said, "and he will have your bird, moreover," answered Jones in quiet triumph.'

In March 1930, a new head keeper, William Robert Bull, arrived from Ireland to take charge of the pheasant shoot. Soon afterwards, in May, he was joined by his twenty-three-year-old son, also William, who continued to live in Llanwddyn until his death and provided much interesting information about the way things were done in those days. As well as the two Bulls, there was a third keeper, who also looked after the foxhounds, which were still kept at the Hotel.

Rearing pheasants was harder work than it has become in more recent years. Eggs were hatched under broody hens, which were put out into a rearing field in wooden coops. Each hen looked after fifteen foster chicks. The coops were set out at twenty-five-yard intervals, the lines of them stretching up the hill towards Ty-Llwyd farm from the bottom of the quarry valley. At six weeks the coops, complete with hen and poults, as the chicks had now become, were taken to be put out in the woods. The hens stayed with their broods until late August or September. After a short time out in the woods, the coops were put up onto wooden stands about five feet high, which meant that the poults had to learn to fly up the roost in the evenings, an important lesson in the process of learning to survive in the wild.

The preparation of food for the young pheasants was a laborious and time-consuming job. The chicks were started on hard-boiled eggs pushed through a sieve. Later they moved onto boiled meat of various sorts mixed with game meal. The big boiler in which all the food was prepared was in a shed at the bottom of the quarry valley. Finally, the well-grown young birds were introduced to their basic diet, wheat.

During the 1930s, the driven pheasant shoot was taken by a syndicate from Birmingham. Graham Martin had a gun in it, in return for his supervision of the shoot and organisation of the shooting days. The party came up every fortnight and shot on two days, either a Friday and Saturday, or a Saturday and the following Monday. Officially two thousand pheasants were reared, but William Bull reckons that his father contrived to make the figure nearer 2500. The best season he remembers was 1934, when the total bag was 1912, a remarkable return considering the numbers released. On 23 November that year, Graham Martin's game-book shows the record score of 412. Then, as now, the shoot was renowned for some spectacular high drives.

In the description of the River Vyrnwy in his book *Wanderings with a Fly-Rod*, Sir Edward Durand breaks off from the subject of fishing to include this paragraph, which starts with mention of a bridge no longer to be found:

'This iron cart-bridge lies just below the covert-clad hilltop, which is called "Garrison Wood", one of the finest stands for high pheasants it has ever been my pleasure to watch.

On the first occasion I saw it driven over the guns, standing in the meadows between it and the river, not one bird of all that came over could have been called an easy shot. I envied each gun in turn as I watched a succession of cocks, looking the size of starlings with long tails, sailing out into the clear air and making for the young plantation on the opposite hill-side, over the river and road.'

In 1934, William Bull was transferred from the pheasant shoot to the moors, where he became assistant to Tom Hughes. Outside the shooting season the moorland keepers' main duty was to wage a constant war on vermin, especially foxes and crows. Whenever the weather was suitable during the months when it was legally permissible, they worked hard to burn as much heather as possible. As the start of the shooting season approached time was spent repairing existing butts and building new ones.

Gadfa moor was reserved for walking-up, as was what was left, after afforestation, of the moor just above the Hotel. Eunant and Allt-Forgan were the main driving moors.

Some idea of the bags on individual days can be given by reference to two sources: the personal game-book of Graham Martin, recently rediscovered in South Africa by his son, and some notes provided by Mr Michael Barker, who was a member of the syndicate that took the driven grouse shooting at Vyrnwy for most of the 1930s.

A few random entries from Graham's game-book give an impression of the sport provided:

August 17, 1932   9 guns on Allt-Forgan shot 43½ brace.
Gorgeous day and shot well.

October 28, 1933   8 guns on Allt-Forgan shot 21 brace.
Devilish cold and unpleasant.

September 1, 1934   8 guns on Gadfa and Eunant shot 20½ brace.
Fine with a few heavy showers.
Gadfa better than usual. Shooting poor.

August 15, 1936   8 guns on Allt-Forgan shot 57½ brace.
In the clouds in the morning, which was
spoilt. Improving in afternoon. Wind
in west.

Michael Barker's notes from three years in the 1930s show what the syndicate achieved. In 1935, they had six days' shooting and shot a total of 242 brace, with a best day of 54½ brace. In 1937, seven days yielded 277 brace, with a best day of seventy-six. Unsurprisingly, the outbreak of war had a disastrous effect on the results for 1939, with only five days and a total bag of 131½ brace, the best day being thirty-six brace on Allt-Forgan on 16 August.

Comparing the syndicate's results with the full total of grouse shot in these years shows that the walking moors must have added considerably to each season's bag. For example, in 1937 there were an additional 130 brace shot over and above those killed on the driving days.

Some of the ponies kept at the Hotel, and praised by J. C. M. Nichols, had an important part to play on the moors. One followed the guns with two panniers slung over its back to carry the game, while another, similarly equipped, brought out the lunch each day. On Allt-Forgan moor there was a wooden lunch hut for use at the Bala end. Ponies were also made available for any guns unable to walk up to their butts to ride to them. The manpower required to provide all the necessary beaters, flankers, pony men and pickers-up was provided partly by the permanent gamekeepers, but also by up to twenty more Corporation men working on the estate. It was possible for the Hotel to have ready call on this source of labour for the pheasant shoot as well as for the grouse moors, under an arrangement worked out with Humphrey Howard.

On 12 August each year the opening of the season was celebrated by a special dinner in the Hotel, the menu for which relied to a great extent on home produced items:

Vyrnwy soup – *usually game*
Vyrnwy trout – *caught in the Lake*
Vyrnwy grouse – *young birds brought down at lunch time from the moors*
Vyrnwy strawberries – *strawberries grown in the garden* and cream
Vyrnwy savoury – *a kind of pâté on wafers*

A good picture of how the whole range of the Hotel's shooting facilities were organised between the wars can be found in a full-page advertisement placed in *Game and Gun* magazine in November 1935. It takes the form of an imaginary letter from a certain Dick, who is writing to his friend Charles, shortly due to return to Britain for a long leave from some outpost of the Empire:

Dear Charles,

I understand you are coming home on leave in November, and that you are anxious to obtain some shooting. I gather that you do not wish to go to the expense of taking your own shoot, with all its ties and responsibilities. A syndicate shoot would probably not appeal to you, with its pre-arranged dates and a fixed sum down. Have you thought of some of the best-known sporting hotels?

I stayed last year at the Lake Vyrnwy Hotel, just over the Welsh border, in the Montgomeryshire mountains. This Hotel has the shooting over 21,000 acres of wonderful sporting country, and six keepers are employed.

During November and December you can get some first-class rough shooting walking-up for 25/- a day. Last year we had some excellent bags up to 25 head, wild pheasants were the principal item, also we got a few grouse, black game, hill partridges, mallard, rabbits, etc. These pheasants, being so often flushed off a steep hillside, give most sporting shots. Some 2000 pheasants are reared annually for a syndicate run by the Hotel (which I gather is fully booked for this year). Naturally some of these birds have spread out over a number of years and have built up a fine head of wild stock. Shooting parties are arranged every other day and are limited to four guns to a party. There are rabbits and pigeons to shoot on odd days, for which there is no charge.

Covert shooting is available to experienced guns on pre-arranged dates; the bags are not large, probably 30 to 40 pheasants, but very high birds are the order of the day. The cost of this is £3 to £4 a day.

The shooting continues throughout January, but is limited to cock pheasants only, which will cost you 10/- a day, and the circumvention of some of those wily old cocks is no mean feat.

If you are in England earlier another year they can provide you with some good grouse shooting. During

August and September there is driving over two moors, where the bags run from 40 to 60 brace on the best moor, and 20 to 30 brace on the smaller moor, prices £4 to £7 a day. This may sound a lot of money, but you must remember that in this country grouse rents are about £1 a brace, and what with beaters' wages, etc., I cannot see how they can do it any cheaper.

Last year I went out on two other moors which they keep for walking-up, and our party had bags up to 10 brace of grouse and a few black game. For this we were charged 25/- a day. It was all very enjoyable. As for the Hotel, it is a nice, warm country house, really well run, and in the winter terms are very moderate. They also have ponies and cobs for riding.

In the spring and summer you would have to go far afield to find better rainbow and brown trout fishing.

I suggest you write direct to the Hotel.

Yrs,
Dick

When war came in 1939, shooting was soon restricted to hunting for the pot. The days of driven grouse and reared pheasants were soon forgotten. William Bull switched from keepering to full-time employment with the Corporation, and the other keepers were diverted to work more productive for the war effort. The few people who continued to go out from time to time with a gun were either too old to have war-time duties, or were officers taking short periods of leave at the Hotel. Such game as they brought back with them was much appreciated in the kitchens.

With the departure of all the keepers, vermin soon established a hold on the countryside. Foxes and crows proliferated, and gradually reduced the grouse stocks almost to vanishing point. Only a few old cock pheasants survived on the lower ground. Because of the depredations of foxes, as well as trapping and occasional shooting by man, even the rabbits were unable to breed successfully enough for their numbers to be maintained at pre-war level.

After the end of the war in 1945, a keeper was once more employed by the Hotel. The first man in the job, named Lloyd, devoted most of his time to killing foxes and trapping rabbits. William Bull remained on the strength of the Liverpool Corporation, but was released at times to help with the fox clearance programme. This was much encouraged throughout the country by a scheme whereby ten shillings was paid for every brush of a fox brought in to certain designated places. In days when, for example, the pay of a recruit for the armed forces was three shillings a day, it can be seen that ten shillings was rather more valuable than it might at first appear.

CHAPTER NINE

Shooting at Lake Vyrnwy:
The Post-War Years

1947–1972

WHEN the Moirs took over the Hotel in March 1947, the sporting part of their lease only covered the low-ground shooting rights. At the instigation of the agent Humphrey Howard, it included among other conditions a limit of five hundred on the number of pheasants that could be reared each season. This was to avoid excessive damage to the arable crops, which were still grown on farms on the estate for feeding stock in the winter, a practice that continued for some years after the war. The grouse moors were let to the Hotel on a different basis, which entailed an annual agreement at an agreed price. Though the Hotel was given first chance to bid for the moors each year, they could have been let to other people if satisfactory agreement had not been reached. This eventuality never, in fact, arose.

Opening a new game-book in 1947, Jamie Moir wrote in it as follows:

'On taking over Lake Vyrnwy Hotel on 8 March 1947 the amount of game on the shootings was negligible, rabbits and wild pheasants having been practically exterminated, but vermin, particularly foxes were present in considerable numbers. It will be of interest to see from this record whether the shooting will be brought back, and how long it will take.'

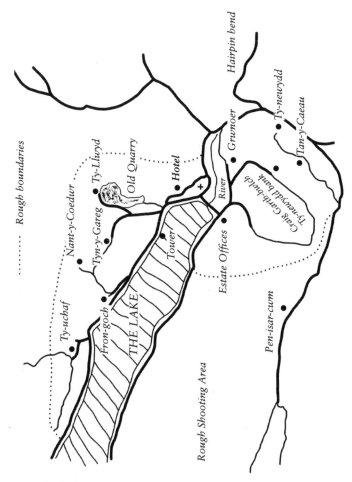

The Pheasant Shoot

To augment the Hotel's own shooting, where Lloyd the keeper continued to direct most of his energies to fox control, Jamie Moir took the shooting rights on several farms lying to the south-east of the Lake, along the road to Llanfyllin. Well on into the 1950s, all these farms had extensive areas of ground under cultivation for corn and root crops, and partridges were plentiful. Two of them, Ceunant and Cammen Fawr, are shown in the game-book to have provided some pleasant, mixed rough shooting in 1954. The season's bag on these two farms comprised forty-eight partridges, thirty pheasants, twenty-four snipe, one duck, twenty-five wood pigeons, two hares, and sixty-six rabbits, mostly shot by Jamie Moir on his own, out for an afternoon with his dogs. On occasions he would be accompanied by one or two guests from the Hotel, or personal friends.

While continuing to rent this shooting on the road to Llanfyllin, and also some other ground to the west of the Lake up the Cownwy valley, Jamie was improving conditions on the Hotel's own shooting, and on the moors. He was putting down one hundred pheasants by this time in the neighbourhood of the Hotel, while the fox killing programme was giving the grouse a chance to recover on the moors. By 1958, there is no mention of Ceunant and Cammen Fawr farms in the game-book, the total bag for the season being almost entirely shot within the Hotel's own rights. It amounted to 129 grouse, seventy-two pheasants, two woodcock, three snipe, five duck, eight wood pigeon, and five hares. The arrival of myxamatosis had by then removed all the rabbits, of which 229 had been killed only two years previously.

Throughout his time at the Hotel, Jamie kept yellow Labradors and bred some very good dogs, which he trained to a high standard. During the winter in the 1950s, when the Hotel was quiet, he went for a walk in the afternoon, with a gun and his dogs, several times a week. For example, in January 1957 the game-book shows that he was out on eleven days, nine times on his own, and twice with one other person. Later, during the

1960s, his name appears less regularly, while there are more mentions of Hotel guests shooting. During this decade, the grouse were making something of a comeback. Bags of over ten brace a day, by six guns walking-up, began to be recorded in the game-book. On 12 August 1970 a party of six shot twenty-two brace at the Cedig end of Allt-Forgan moor, the best single day's bag since 1939, and unlikely ever to be improved upon again.

1972–1987

During the weekend marking the retirement of Jamie Moir and the arrival of my family and I, one of the activities laid on was a short day's grouse driving on Eunant moor on 28 October 1972. Although limitations on time available only allowed for three drives, a good number of birds were seen, and 12½ brace were shot. All arrangements for the day depended on William Bull, who had previously given me a guided tour of all the moors, and shown me all the old lines of butts, and the ways to reach them. On this day he had collected a good team of beaters, and directed them with skill, making full use of all the knowledge he had absorbed as a young moorkeeper well over thirty years previously. The season's bag of grouse for 1972 was 88½ brace.

The following year our shooting efforts were again concentrated on the moors, with only one hundred pheasants turned into covert. In the game-book, I wrote some notes on the 1973–74 season, during which the number of grouse shot was 111½ brace, the highest total from 1939 until today, and alas likely to remain so. My notes read as follows:

> 'The grouse season opened with a period of hot sunny weather, which lasted well into the second week. The stock of birds was about average, with quite a number of cheepers seen. These must have been second broods following some unusually heavy thunderstorms in late

May at the time of hatching, which must have caused a certain amount of damage.

A feature of August was the number of hen barriers seen over the moors, particularly to the north-east of the Lake over Allt-Forgan. The tendency was for the grouse to be driven away from the tops to the fringes of the moors. How much the stock of grouse was actually depleted by the harriers is hard to know, but they were certainly moved from some of the areas where they were expected to be found.

As apparently often happens in this part of Wales, the grouse seemed to be more plentiful as the season progressed. But this may well have been merely due to a lot of birds having sat very tight early on in the hot weather, and only showing themselves later in the season. A driving day was held on Allt-Forgan on 6 October. A lot of birds were seen, though they were strong, wild, and far from easy to shoot!'

Special mention was accorded to 6 October because, on all the other twenty days that year on which parties went out, they walked-up the birds and it was the only time driving was attempted. During the following four seasons, more frequent driving days were organised but were not often very successful. Eleven brace on Gadfa on 21 September 1974 was one of the better bags achieved. All too often remarks in the game-book include comments such as 'fiendish weather – gales and rain', or 'strong wind and very wet'. As an alternative, the weather was recorded on 14 November 1975 as fine with an east wind, but the small bag on Allt-Forgan was put down to a different reason: 'A good show of birds on the last two drives, but marksmanship not as good as it might have been.'

The totals of grouse shot each year held up reasonably well until 1977. At the end of that season I wrote in the game-book that: 'The grouse were a puzzle in 1977. At the beginning of the season there did not seem to be many about, but by the end of September there were quite a lot.' I went on to explain that the decision had been made to cut down the amount of walking-up in August, and then recorded the story of a driving day rained off on 24 September. However, my notes ended confidently:

> 'The next week on Gadfa wind and rain, and sometimes hail, came as well. But the stock of birds was remarkable, and on the first drive we saw a great many. Several coveys broke back, but even so we got four brace at that one drive, all coming like rockets.'

On 8 October we had a very good day. We could only manage four drives, as cloud on the hill delayed our start. Again, the birds were hard to hit, and the total bag of thirteen brace does not really indicate the very healthy numbers seen.

The following year, 1978, saw the start in the downturn in the grouse stock, which has never picked up again during the succeeding years. At the end of the entries in the game-book this note was inserted:

> 'The 1978 grouse season can only be described as disastrous. The total bag was only 46½ brace, and we shot far too many old birds in this number compared to young ones.

> Where the grouse have disappeared to is a mystery, as both Gadfa and Eunant moors carried very good stocks at the end of 1977. However, all moors around the Vyrnwy area seem to be in the same state.

It remains to be seen whether we can allow any shooting
at all on the moors in 1979. If the early walking-up days
in August show that there is a serious shortage of birds we
will have to cancel the later days.'

During 1979 and 1980, Eunant continued to produce some quite
good days, but little could be found on Gadfa and Allt-Forgan,
both of which moors were only visited once. Throughout the
1980s the pattern remained the same, though occasionally signs
of recovery in certain places made us think that an upturn in
numbers might be underway. For example, on 31 August 1985,
a day with two drives on Gadfa and two on Eunant produced
12½ brace, with enough birds seen to have shot twenty brace
with better marksmanship. Those two moors were left alone
apart from that one day, but in spite of this there was once again
a shortage in 1986. Since then we have shot the three moors
more and more lightly, but it has made little difference: the steady
decline in numbers has gone on inexorably.

It was an attempt to find ways of combating this steady
decrease in our stock that a seminar was held in the Hotel on 25
March 1982 to discuss 'The Decline of Red Grouse in Wales'.
The late Sir Watkin Williams-Wynn was in the chair, and expert
speakers addressed a sizeable audience of moor owners and
tenants, syndicate members, gamekeepers and what might be
termed occasional grouse shooters. In all, nearly ninety people
crowded into the big drawing room in the Hotel. The proceedings
were extensively written up in *The Field* by Dick Orton, and in
The Shooting Times by John Buckland. I made a brief summary
of the day's findings, from which the following paragraphs have
been extracted:

'Grouse have declined in numbers in Wales since a peak in
1915. This was to be expected during the two World Wars,
and after each a revival took place, though figures never

again came near the 1915 level. The big worry is that the revival from 1950 to 1975 has not been sustained, and from 1978 onwards nearly all Welsh moors have shown a steady downward trend.

The three causes of this decline are common to other parts of the country, but their effect in Wales is more pronounced than elsewhere due to the poor grouse habitat provided by most of the hill land. High rainfall, poor quality shale subsoil and, consequently, slow re-generating and easily destroyed heather have always made the grouse population in Wales smaller than that found in the north of England and much of Scotland.

The three main causes themselves are the spread of forestry, excessive grazing by sheep often accompanied by careless farming methods, and the attacks of ever-increasing numbers of vermin, especially foxes and crows. When these harmful factors are all found together, grouse are in danger of extinction. The smaller the stock of birds on a moor, the greater the danger becomes.

The only way to restore the situation is by good management. This entails systematic, well-organised heather burning, control of sheep stocks, and good keepering. Given the will and the resources to manage a moor well, there is no reason why one in Wales should not hold a sufficient head of grouse to provide reasonable sport, in spite of the fact that the habitat is not good enough to sustain stocks such as are known in other parts of Britain.

Unfortunately, on many Welsh moors the situation may have been reached where the will and the resources to restore the grouse are lacking. There are too few gamekeepers, and those that there are usually spend most of their energies looking after pheasants. Furthermore, when grouse have become scarce, it takes a long time to build them up again, and there is no return in the short-term for the time and money that has to be devoted to the necessary work. But unless something is done, it is more than likely that eventually grouse in Wales will become extinct.

Above all, we must actually DO something to put matters right. There is no point in talking endlessly about the problems unless action is taken to solve them. It is sincerely hoped that everyone who can help in any way will make the effort to stop the steady decline of the grouse in Wales towards its all-too-possible extinction.'

Although everyone departed full of resolve to do something, this was to prove easier said than done. As John Buckland pointed out in his article, 'management is expensive, clearly very expensive if conducted ideally', and this factor above all others is the one that has prevented a full-scale effort to restore the grouse population in Wales.

In the years where it was possible, due to drier than normal weather, we worked hard at Vyrnwy to burn as much heather as could be tackled within the legal time limits. However, due to the extent of the moors, the proportion burnt was always relatively small. As far as vermin control is concerned, the main effort was directed towards keeping down the number of foxes, both through the activities of the local foxhounds and by killing cubs in the summer. Crows were less easy to deal with, and were present in greater numbers than desirable. To do much more than was done already would mean a massive injection of money and labour over a period of years, at the end of which there would be no guarantee that grouse stocks would be noticeably greater.

It would have been a bigger gamble than anyone was likely to take.

The gradual build-up of the pheasant shoot at Vyrnwy began in 1974. Instead of just putting down a hundred poults in the Hotel grounds, as had been Jamie Moir's practice for many years, we decided to double that number and put them out on the shoot, in a release pen in a young wood near Tyn-y-gareg farm. The site was chosen in conjunction with William Bull, my valued adviser and part-time head keeper throughout much of the 1970s. On his advice we asked Trevor Hill, a member of the well-known local family mentioned earlier in the book, to build the pen for us. Trevor was a man of great practical skill and intelligence, as well as enormous physical strength, but few words. I gave him the Game Conservancy (now Game & Wildlife Conservation Trust) pamphlet describing how to build a release pen to work from, and he took it from me with a nod. When the work was finished the pen was a masterpiece, constructed exactly to the specification in the pamphlet. To help him Trevor had obtained the assistance of a forester on the estate called Brian Roberts, who was to play an important role in the shoot in future.

As the years went by, the number of pheasants released was steadily increased and more pens were built. Valuable help came from a Game Conservancy advisory visit by Christopher Minchin. Our average return on numbers put down was over fifty per cent: for example, 207 out of 400 in 1977, and 279 out of 500 in 1979. In 1981 we were up to 1000 released, with 473 shot. By 1985 we were up to 2500 put down with a return of over fifty per cent at 1313 shot, but were nearer the national average the following season, with a total bag of only 1156 from the same number released to covert.

As the shoot was enlarged, more drives were opened up, some being ones remembered by William Bull and others from pre-1939 days, and some developed on likely looking bits of ground. Shooting took place regularly once a week, with bags eventually reaching 100 to 130 in November and early December, and 60 to 80 later in the season. Throughout these years there was no full-time keeper. When William Bull decided to reduce his involvement, Gwyn Jones took over, assisted by George Jones, having recently retired from working on the estate as a blacksmith. Gwyn, known as 'Gwyn the Fox' because he ran the local hounds, was with us for three years before leaving the area, to be followed by Brian Roberts.

1987 – today

When he took over the Hotel in February 1987, Jim Bisiker created the Vyrnwy Sporting Company and appointed his son Brian as the sporting manager, with the major responsibility of greatly extending the amount of shooting available each season. In another important step in this direction, the sporting lease was re-negotiated with the Severn Trent Water Authority. The moors became part of the overall sporting lease, whereas in 1972 they were taken on on an annual basis, the twenty-one-year lease of those days was replaced by a fifty year one, and the limit on the number of pheasants put down raised from five hundred to 8500 each year. The Hotel also extended its sporting acreage by purchasing the outright ownership of the sporting rights of the moor known as Mynydd St John, lying on the south-west side of the Lake, up the Cownwy valley. These eight thousand acres include low ground in the valley as well as the heather moorland.

For the first season under new management, Sir John Baynes, accompanied by Lady Baynes, who came picking-up with her dogs to every shoot, took charge of the guns on shooting days, and Brian Bisiker understudied him to learn his way around the various parts of the shoot. This was only intended to last for one season but the warm working relationship that developed between them both lasted until Sir John's death in 2005. Brian Roberts was also taken on full-time as the head keeper, a position he filled with great ability, building on the work that he and his wife Mabel had done on a part-time basis and in their free time to build up the shoot before taking up his permanent post in 1987.

An immediate increase was made in the number of pheasants put down, with the result that the 1987–88 season's total bag was two and a half times larger than in 1986–87. Further increases the following year brought the figure up to the approximate level at which it then remained for the rest of the century, a development that was greatly assisted by additional keepers being appointed to assist Brian Roberts. This expansion and development, combined with the maintenance of Vyrnwy's warm hospitality and traditional approach to shooting, led to the shoot achieving a reputation for excellence and well-deserved popularity.

In 1997, Brian Roberts retired as Head Keeper and John Roberts was appointed in his place. The shoot became more focused at this time, as the Hotel started to cater for other sporting interests by developing clay pigeon shooting. When Brian Bisiker was appointed Managing Director of the Hotel in 1999, John took over as the sporting manager in addition to being Head Keeper, dual roles which he holds to this day. The first clay range was built by Brian in 1987 since when it has moved and been enhanced three times so that today it boasts an impressive, fully-automated layout.

Sadly, the prospects for grouse in Wales in the 1990s were not good and this has remained the case ever since. On the three days small parties went out on the Vyrnwy moors in 1991, very few birds were seen. Reports from other places were depressingly similar. Heather burning was stopped at this time and a mowing programme introduced instead. Since then, there has been no organised grouse shooting at Vyrnwy and only occasional guns walking-up on the moors. That said, there are still blackcock on the moors, which represent the most southerly black grouse in the UK.

It would be fair to claim that the pheasant shoot at Lake Vyrnwy ranked then as it does today as among the finest in the country. The quality of the birds shown is matched by the beauty of the scenery, while the comfort of the Hotel adds to the pleasure of the sport. On two separate occasions at the end of a day, a gun said to Sir John that he had just experienced the best day's shooting he had ever known. Brian Roberts and his successor John Roberts both perfected the art of showing high pheasants at their best. To watch the birds drifting off the hill above Ty-Llwyd farm, or rocketing out over the valley from Garrison wood, or sailing out from the Tyn-y-Gareg oaks, or indeed flying from numerous other coverts, is to see some of the finest and most testing shooting to be found anywhere in the world.

Epilogue

THE future for Lake Vyrnwy Hotel and its surrounding estate looks brighter today than it has for a long time. This is a tribute to Brian Bisiker and his team who have put the Hotel on a firm footing for the future and to Severn Trent who, through the newly established Welsh part of their business named Hafren Dyfrdwy, have reversed their previous policy of disengagement from the Vyrnwy valley and instead decided to invest for the long-term. This book has described the changes that have been made by Brian Bisiker and his management team but has also shown that the charm which characterised the Hotel under the Moirs and my father, Sir John Baynes, has been preserved.

When I was the County Councillor for Llanwddyn between 2008 and 2012, I saw at close quarters the extreme instability caused by Severn Trent putting the Vyrnwy estate up for sale. I organised a series of public meetings with the local community that gave voice not only to their concerns but also their strong feeling that Severn Trent should see Vyrnwy as an asset not a liability. It is rare for a public company to listen to ordinary people but to their credit Severn Trent in the form of Hafren Dyfrdwy has done just that and recently unveiled substantial investment plans for the future. Looking back, it is now clear that the attempted sale was a catalyst for change at Vyrnwy not only in the policies of Severn Trent but also the local community, which has become much more active and cohesive than ten years ago.

Hafren Dyfrdwy unveiled in September 2018 an investment plan for Lake Vyrnwy of nearly £2 million, which will be spent on what the company describes as the 'visitor experience' as well as on restoring 450 hectares of upland peat bogs near the Lake. The blanket bogs above Lake Vyrnwy are one of the most important areas for wildlife and nature in Wales, earning them the highest levels of special designation including being a Site of Special Scientific Interest (SSSI), one of several SSSIs on the Vyrnwy estate. Hafren Dyfrdwy said that the overall investment project will increase the number of people who visit and stay in and near the Vyrnwy valley, thus improving the local economy.

The scheme has secured £1.5 million of Heritage Lottery Funding of which nearly £300,000 is to be spent on the joint RSPB Cymru – Hafren Dyfrdwy Lake Vyrnwy Experience project. This aims to make Lake Vyrnwy – already home to rare breeds including hen harrier, black grouse and merlin – an even better home for wildlife through work not only to protect the rare upland bog but also ancient woodland. It will also entail redevelopment of Bethel Chapel near the dam as a visitor centre and restoration work to attractions around the Lake such as the sculpture park, picnic areas and walking trails. The money is a development grant that will enable RSPB Cymru – Hafren Dyfrdwy to apply for a full grant in 2020 and identify opportunities for employment, training and volunteering to support farming and conservation work at Vyrnwy.

I wanted, however, to finish this book with some thoughts on the essentials of hotel management, the successful pursuit of which explains the continued success of Lake Vyrnwy Hotel today. They are a combination of my father's comments from the first edition of this book (the wisdom of which my three brothers and I saw at first-hand growing up and helping out at the Hotel) followed by the thoughts of Anthony Rosser who, alongside Brian Bisiker, has managed the Hotel with great success since 2000. Both express timeless truths about how to treat visitors well, ensure their comfort and enjoyment and therefore their return visits.

Simon Baynes

Sir John Baynes, 1992

There is a well-known saying, attributed to Conrad Hilton, that the three prime requisites for a successful hotel are: 'Location, location, location'. Certainly, one established in an unsuitable location will never be a success, however well run, so being situated in the right place is a first essential. Other obvious requirements include adequate warmth; plenty of hot water; pleasant, though not necessarily luxurious, interior decoration; and, in modern times, bedrooms with their own private bathrooms and lavatories. All sections of the building and its contents, needless to say, must be kept thoroughly clean.

Assuming that all these requirements have been met, there are three vital factors that decide whether a hotel is a really good one or just run-of-the-mill. These are (not in order of priority as all are of equal importance) the efficiency of the reception system, the standard of the food, and the manners of the staff.

It took me a very long time to realise the importance of the reception system, which covers all aspects of a guest's contact with a hotel from a first tentative telephone call to handing over a bill, and saying good-bye, at the end of a visit. It was a charming German lady travel writer who brought home to me in conversation the significance of this aspect. She pointed out that a person who had been received on arrival with a really efficient and friendly welcome would excuse almost any fault in a hotel, while nothing would be right for someone whose arrival had been met with muddle or surly indifference. While it is easy to point out this irrefutable fact, it is not quite so simple to ensure that a reception office is always able to handle matters correctly.

The first problem is concerned with time. Guests require attention from, say, 7am until about 11pm even in a country hotel. To have efficient, properly rested people on duty for 16 hours a day is a considerable strain on the resources of even a large, urban establishment; for a small to medium-size place in a rural area it is a constant problem. Apart from finding the people to do the work satisfactorily, the long period to be covered each day means that paying those who can be found is expensive. If expense is avoided by trusting to anyone who is available to answer telephones or meet arrivals, there is always the risk of failing to provide that standard of welcome that has just been shown to be so vital.

Handling telephone enquiries is much more complicated than it might appear. To start with, a caller expects a reasonably quick response, and if one does not come after a long series of rings he or she may give up in disgust, and a valuable bit of business may be lost. Indeed, the opportunities to lose good bookings by inefficient answering of the telephone are much greater than might be imagined. To avoid such slips, the person taking a call must answer swiftly and politely; must be able to give availability of rooms and prices without too much delay; and must remember to record all necessary information about the customer's own details and exact requirements. While reservations by letter are more satisfactory, there is often not time for these, nor even to write in confirmation of a telephone booking, so what is dealt with verbally must avoid all error. This is much easier said than done.

In looking after the guest while actually staying in a hotel, the people working in the reception area will have many odd things to do that cannot be elaborated upon here, but are generally obvious. At the end of the stay comes the moment most fraught with the possibility of destroying a heretofore pleasant relationship – the presentation of the bill. Errors in favour of the hotel are usually noticed immediately, while those in favour of the customer sometimes go unmarked. Those most often found in the former category include failure to record a deposit made in advance, or charging a rate different to one originally quoted. Having to apologise for such errors, and correct them, is a galling business, which has to be done with the best grace possible while inwardly cursing oneself or one's staff for being so stupid.

There is no need to give further examples of ways in which a first-class reception system is of such consequence in running a good hotel. It took me a long time to wake up to this obvious fact, and I suspect many proprietors and managers around the country never do so. It must be remembered, however, that it is far from easy to achieve, and must be constantly worked at. In this respect it has much in common with the next essential to discuss, which is the maintenance of a good standard of food.

In catering, the key word is consistency, not with reference to the texture of the product, but in respect of its quality, and the promptitude with which it is served. My personal preference is for simple meals, and I believe that a country hotel does best to stick to uncomplicated menus of straightforward, traditional dishes. Apart from the fact that I would far rather be offered a short menu of simple choices than be handed an elaborate bill of fare expressed in high-flown, fancy language, there are many advantages in being slightly unsophisticated. It is much more likely that a limited number of dishes will be really well cooked and flavoured than will be the case if a big selection is offered. While not necessarily the case, and there are clearly examples where this statement does not apply, the facilities of the average country hotel favour a restricted number of alternatives. What is more, it is possible to ensure that the guests being served with the food can receive each course without undue delay.

The strain of providing first-class meals at regular intervals throughout the day on seven days a week, and of ensuring that they are deftly and pleasantly served, should never be underestimated. Because of this strain, it is wise to avoid being over-ambitious, but to concentrate on supplying a consistent standard of meals at the best level the hotel's facilities will allow. The situation has been eased to some extent in recent years as the demand for luncheons of three or more courses has virtually disappeared, except for people celebrating some special event. The provision of a simple cold buffet, or bar meals, is now generally considered adequate in a country hotel. Many guests will probably want picnic lunches, and although the preparation of these takes the strain off the kitchen, it requires a good deal of effort and imagination to come up with a really attractive end product. Where there is always a big demand for picnics, no short cuts should be taken in preparing them.

What to do about tea is a problem. Some places do not provide it at all these days, some only provide tea and biscuits, while a few still offer a traditional full spread of toast, sandwiches, cake and so on. The value of serving teas is to be found in terms of goodwill rather than for any financial gain. The sort of prices that can be charged are never sufficient to cover the cost of preparing teas and paying staff to serve them, but every now and then new guests will return to stay as residents having originally been inspired by a short visit just for tea.

The two meals at which a hotel must maintain the highest possible standards are breakfast and dinner. The temptation to cut corners over arrangements for breakfast is all too often resisted less fiercely than it should be. A certain amount of self-service from a well set up side-board is acceptable, but thin, tinned fruit juice and butter and marmalade in horrible little plastic containers are most certainly not. To cook and serve delicious, substantial breakfasts is just as demanding a task as providing any other meal, requiring as much, if not more, attention to detail.

In discussing dinner, the first thing to establish is the difference between a restaurant and a hotel dining room. Usually the former goes with a large establishment in an urban or suburban setting, and deliberately encourages the presence of customers other than residents. The latter, while usually open to non-residents, is geared to the requirements of people staying in the hotel, and is what is normally found in places in country settings. A restaurant will probably serve dinner from 7 to 10pm, and will offer both a set and an à la carte menu. The staff running it will work under different conditions to those involved in a dining room, where dinner will be available for a much shorter period of time, and on a much less extensive scale. My own personal experience relates only to a dining room, where dinner was served at a set time. I believe this to be the most suitable arrangement for a small place in a rural area, especially when local staff from the surrounding neighbourhood are employed.

In respect of the menu provided in a dining room, I return to the earlier plea for simplicity, and suggest a series of choices in threes. To start, soup, pâté and one other alternative; next, one red meat dish, one of white meat, and one of fish; then, three types of pudding; and finally, three English and three French cheeses on a board. To send in a well-cooked dinner in this range of variety is enough to tax the skill of any chef or cook working with limited assistance and facilities.

Having expressed these personal preferences, I must admit that the restaurant now operating at Lake Vyrnwy provides dinners of outstanding quality, which I am always hearing praised in glowing terms, both by residents and casual visitors. They are, however, an exceptional team, and their unusual range of ability is unlikely to be found in the average country hotel. For this reason, I still believe that running a dining room with a simple range of menus is the best answer for most such establishments.

As important as the quality of the food is the way in which it is served, which brings me to the third of the three vital factors mentioned at the start of the chapter, namely the manners of the staff. The ideal to be sought after is the creation of an unhurried atmosphere of quiet efficiency, in which all the guests' requirements are met with a cheerful willingness and a minimum of fuss. To get the correct balance, so that annoying over-attentiveness or excessive obsequiousness are avoided, and yet there is no hint of carelessness or undue familiarity, is something that must be worked at constantly. The lead must come from the top, with the owner or manager personally demonstrating the correct attitude towards the guests, and also watching to ensure that the staff follow his or her example.

As far as possible, everyone should enjoy doing the job well. The right outlook for those working in the hotel business at all levels was well described in a television programme I once saw about a man who was starting up a new country pub. Talking to his newly recruited staff just before the opening day, he told them that he wanted their jobs to be fun for them, stressing at the same time: 'Fun, but not a joke.' It makes a useful motto for engendering the right spirit into the staff of any hotel, but is especially valuable in relation to a small, rural establishment where a friendly atmosphere is so essential.

Inevitably an explanation of these three important aspects of hotel management sounds trite, and obvious, when set down in this way. However, though there may be nothing very original in what I have written, I can guarantee that any hotel that provides a warm welcome, consistently good, simple food, and well-mannered service will never fail to have plenty of satisfied customers.

Anthony Rosser, 2019

There is much wisdom in Sir John's thoughts on the running of a good country hotel. In some ways nothing much has really changed at Vyrnwy: the generations rumble on and each new one seems to want something different to the last. The practices of competent communication and business efficiency are as relevant today as they were before, just done a little differently.

In 1985, there were thirty bedrooms that welcomed just over 5400 overnight visitors, most of whom stayed for several nights or even a week or two. The Hotel closed for a period of time at the end of shooting season and re-opened in time for the fishing.

In 2019, there are fifty-two bedrooms and around 26,000 overnight guests sleep in the Hotel, staying for an average of 1.4

nights. The business runs for 364½ days per year, closing only for one evening to give the staff a well-earned party.

The bookings now come in different ways: the reception team cannot actually remember the last time a reservation request came by post and the receipt of payment by cheque is now an event to be remarked upon.

Over seventy per cent of bookings come over the internet, going directly into the property management computer system with no human intervention, a system that alters rates and distribution world-wide automatically. Many guests have no interaction with the Hotel when making a reservation apart from through their computer and, increasingly, their mobile phone.

The telephone, however, remains the lifeblood of the hotel reception. There are of course other methods of communication: email is a dominant force and the aged fax machine, not a feature in 1985, is still used by one supplier. Social media in all its forms now make our affairs very public with review sites changing the very thinking in our business lives. These may challenge us at times but they also offer opportunities to the seasoned operator. The fact that we now live our lives and conduct our business online is a concept that would be completely alien and threatening to the hotelier of the 1980s.

The principles of good hospitality, however, remain the same. Lots of hot water is a necessity but guests no longer share bathrooms down the corridor and, where once the provision of a bath *and* a shower was a significant luxury, it is now a fundamental requirement, as are digital television sets with a plethora of channels. Telephones, however, have almost been and gone. Good WiFi to some is actually more important than fresh air and the present patchy signal on the local mobile network is to some a tragedy of the first order. Many more, however, are delighted and relieved at the rest from the hubbub.

Heating throughout the day and night is a given, and health and safety has banned hot water bottles. The generations of experienced mothers and grandmothers from the village no longer babysit for guests' children, unless they are on the correct register and have proper childcare training and insurance.

'Manners maketh man': Sir John's simple advice on providing relaxed elegance and the politeness of staff is as important today as it ever was. The un-stuffy welcoming and friendly service he describes was enlightened thinking from a man who was quite formal himself and from a very different age. His thoughts on proper country house cooking and understanding what a guest wants are well made and continue to be relevant in a world of international cuisine where younger people eat what and when they want.

We no longer serve dinner *en masse* at the stroke of a gong but at times in the depth of the season it may feel like it. Now food is available 24 hours a day with the restaurant clinging to the last vestiges of formality and a more contemporary brasserie serving more casual fare. Only a few years ago over eighty per cent of hotel guests would eat formally in the restaurant; now the move to more casual dining and flexible eating times has moved the mix to fifty:fifty, and it is inevitable that this trend will continue.

Fundamentally, Sir John's rules for keeping a good house have changed little, and there are many less grounded in the traditional values of our great industry that could benefit from spending time reading his wise words.

Acknowledgements

WE must start by paying tribute to the present owners, the Bisiker family, and the management of the Hotel for their support in the preparation and distribution of this book.

Many people have helped us to trace the story of the Hotel by giving us their own personal reminiscences or putting us in touch with useful sources of information and they are mentioned accordingly in the book. We are extremely grateful to them and any other people we might have forgotten, to whom we extend our apologies for not mentioning them by name.

Several published journals and books have been of particular importance and these include the following: *The Montgomeryshire Collections*, Volumes VI and VII (1873 and 1874); *Wanderings with a Fly-Rod*, by Sir Edward Durand (1938); *Notes on Trout Fishing in Lake Vyrnwy and the Upper Vyrnwy River*, by R. E. Threlfall (1947); *Lake Vyrnwy and Around*, by W. M. Gallichan (1912); *History and Description of Llanwddyn and Lake Vyrnwy*, by D. W. L. Rowlands (1972); *Angling Holidays in pursuit of Salmon, Trout and Pike*, by C. W. Gedney (1896).